DD//L   7.9%

MW01089508

DATE DUE

MAY 1 8 1998 JUN 0 9 1998			

641.62
Ber

TRADER VIC'S
RUM COOKERY AND DRINKERY

BOOKS BY TRADER VIC

TRADER VIC'S RUM COOKERY AND DRINKERY
TRADER VIC'S BOOK OF MEXICAN COOKING
FRANKLY SPEAKING: TRADER VIC'S OWN STORY
THE MENEHUNES
TRADER VIC'S BOOK OF FOOD AND DRINK
TRADER VIC'S BARTENDER'S GUIDE, *Revised*
TRADER VIC'S PACIFIC ISLAND COOKBOOK

DEDICATED to those wonderful distillers of rum who have contributed so much to the pleasure of living by making not just one kind of rum, but a great variety of rums—so that all can enjoy this fantastic liquor.

TRADER VIC'S RUM COOKERY AND DRINKERY

BY VICTOR J. BERGERON

ASSISTED BY SHIRLEY SARVIS

ILLUSTRATIONS BY JANE WALWORTH

GARDEN CITY, NEW YORK

DOUBLEDAY & COMPANY, INC.

1974

Library of Congress Cataloging in Publication Data

Bergeron, Victor Jules.
    Trader Vic's rum cookery and drinkery.

    1. Cookery (Rum) 2. Alcoholic beverages.
I. Sarvis, Shirley, joint author. II. Title.
III. Title: Rum cookery and drinkery.
TX726.B44   641.6′2
ISBN 0-385-04108-X
Library of Congress Catalog Card Number 72–96261

Printed in the United States of America
First Edition

CONTENTS

TRADER VIC'S
RUM COOKERY AND DRINKERY

TO BEGIN WITH

Fifteen men on a dead man's chest, yo-ho-ho and a bottle of rum. And that's the same old stuff that's been written a thousand times. It's not what I'm going to do in this book; I am not going to rehash everything that has been written about rum. Nor am I going to tell you about how it was drunk by pirates and Creole chippies and stumble bums and about the Green Mountain Boys who took a shot of rum to get started on their chores or how Paul Revere got half tanked up on rum so that he could shout, "The British are coming!" from Boston to Lexington without taking a breath. If you want the ancient data, you can buy some history books. I'm mostly going to talk about the twentieth century, not way back when.

Here I intend to give you a twentieth-century roundup of rum—what it is, how it is made, where it is made, the many varieties of rum, and the many ways you can use rum in drinks and cooking.

Rum is the most delightful liquor distilled, and it comes in a lot of varieties—light, dark, medium-dark, strong-flavored, mild-flavored—all wonderful stuff.

Rum and rum making have changed a lot in the last twenty years. When Trader Vic's first started out in business, there were thirty-five or forty rums in back of our bar. Most rums then were very strong, potent, high in proof, and varied in quality. Some were acceptable, some were not. Today, there are available more than a hundred registered brand names of rum, plus all the private labels. (In one little town in Germany there are twenty-nine distilleries busily turning out many varieties of rum.) There are a lot more light rums than before. The making of rum is much more controlled.

But today, in our Trader Vic bars, we stock perhaps twenty rums, because most Americans keep right on asking for scotch, Bourbon, or gin, even when attending a cocktail party on a Caribbean island. Americans haven't yet learned to enjoy rum. I think that the main reason for this is that rum has never really been a liquor that American people bought and drank as a habit. Rum has always been sort of a special thing, and scotch, gin, Bourbon, and vodka are the liquors that are regularly drunk, and that's it.

I used to drink a lot of rum, and I made rum drinks both at home and in my restaurant. Then when I could afford to have help run our house, I gradually got away from serving rum. I can remember people coming to our house and asking for a Mai Tai, and I would look at them kind of funny. And there is the story in a nutshell: Most of the time we just don't *think* of using rum.

So here in this book we are going to go about doing just that.

Rum is just one helluva liquor to drink. And if people don't drink it because it isn't supposed to be sophisticated, that still doesn't say that it isn't good. On one recent night, I was negotiating a new restaurant with some people from Japan, and I had five or six old-fashioneds made with Mai Tai rum. I felt swell the next day, and I couldn't say that if I'd been drinking Bourbon, scotch, gin, or vodka.

You will get more enjoyment and pleasure out of drinking rum than any liquor I know.

Now a word about the cookery part of the book. This is a rum cookbook.

But let's thoroughly understand one thing. This is not a cookbook where rum is put into a lot of food just for the hell of it. Just to put rum—or brandy or wine—into food doesn't necessarily make it good; you have got to know what you are doing. Every damn one of the recipes in this book has been made for a long time. Each has been developed by people who know what they are doing. These recipes will work, and they are among the best ones you can find anywhere.

Try them if they look good to you. I think you will enjoy them.

I suppose everybody knows, but for those who don't: Rum is a distillation of products of the sugar cane. The story of rum making is the fascinating story of how sweet, juicy sugar cane is transformed into a distinctive alcoholic beverage.

There is some rum production practically every place that sugar cane is grown. So, many places in the world produce rum—the Hawaiian Islands, Australia, South Africa, Mexico, the Philippines, all of the islands of the West Indies, South America. And plenty of places that don't grow sugar cane produce rum from sugar cane products that are shipped in: New England in the United States, the Bordeaux area of France, Germany, England.

We don't know the exact date, but it seems that the first important rum was produced in Barbados in 1647 shortly after the island was settled. It was first known as "killdevil," and I suppose that is where the name "devil rum" started. Then, after a short time, it was known as "rum bouillon," and by 1667 it was called plain, ordinary "rum."

Rum can be made from molasses or pure sugar juice crushed out of the cane or both. Most rum today is made from molasses.

The Basic Process

Sugar cane that has grown to full maturity is harvested and taken to the factory for processing. There it travels by conveyor belt to the choppers, where it is washed and cut into small pieces, and then to the crushers, where the juice is first squeezed. The cane then passes through rollers, which separate the juice from the pulp. (The pulp, known as bagasse, is taken off to become fuel or to be made into other products.) Some rum makers use this fresh-squeezed juice as the starting point for rum making; at this point it is piped to the distillery. Others continue working with the juice to separate out the molasses: The juice is boiled at high temperatures so that important changes occur in its glucose and sucrose content. The sucrose forms into sugar crystals, and the glucose turns into molasses. The heavy, sticky molasses syrup is separated from the sugar and piped to the distillery.

The molasses or the pressed cane juice is mixed with a proportion of water and yeast to become the "wash." The wash is pumped into fermentation vats where it is left for about twenty-four hours for the fermentation to take place (the basic fermentation process is the yeast converting the sugar content to alcohol and carbon dioxide; the carbon dioxide passes off as a gas). During fermentation, these chemical compounds are produced: aldehydes, esters, ethyl alcohol, and fusel oil. (The aldehydes, esters, and fusel oil are the congeners that give rum its major flavor. Ethyl alcohol is of neutral flavor.) These compounds are then removed from the water of the fermentation batch by distillation. This distillation is possible because of the simple fact that alcohol and congeners both boil at a lower temperature than water. Distillation boils off the alcohol and these various congeners, separating them off at their various boiling points. The so-called purest distillation is pure ethyl alcohol; its flavor is neutral. Less complete distillations can include some or all of the congeners and thus produce a distillation product that is highly flavorful.

The distillation process can be effected by either a pot (kettle) still or a column (continuous) still. The product resulting from pot still distillation is less precisely measured off and separated than in the continuous still, so it contains more of the flavoring congeners. The product resulting from a continuous still can be precisely separated out to delineate the particular flavoring congeners; and it can become a lighter and more delicately flavored product, or even so clean of congeners as to be pure alcohol and flavorless. Many rum makers use the products of both the pot and the continuous stills and blend them.

Immediately after distillation, rum, like all alcoholic spirits, is water-white. This rum is put into barrels (usually forty-gallon oak) for aging. This aging may go on for as little as one year to as much as twenty. During aging, the wood lends flavor and color to the rum. The rum maker may then blend various rums to achieve his desired result.

Every rum area has its own style, and every rum maker has his own way of handling all of these processes. Every variation has an effect on the eventual end-product rum characteristics: flavor, body, color, aroma, sweetness or dryness, acidity. . . .

RUMS

FROM DIFFERENT ISLANDS
AND FAR-OFF PLACES

Each important rum island produces a lot of rum and a lot of different qualities of rums in order to satisfy its own local market and its various export markets. A Martinique rum maker, for example, is perfectly capable and willing to produce a beautiful, smooth, brandylike aged rum for the connoisseurs of Martinique; a young, rough, harsh, overproof white rum for the country or peasant or poorer of the population; a silky, smooth white rum for the making of *the* local rum drink, petit punch; a dark, molassey deep-flavored rum for export to France (for use in winter hot grog drinks and for pastry flavoring); a nearly pure alcohol vodkalike white rum for export to Germany; and a dark rum for the United States.

Such is true in every rum country. There are many rums produced for the local market and for export elsewhere which we never see in this country. Most rum makers produce the rums to be exported to the United States according to their own estimation of what will sell well in the United States and according to our import law requirements.

Yet, we in the United States can somewhat classify rums by point of origin, because the rums that come to us from various areas do show fairly marked distinctions. These United States import rums (the ones you can find in your liquor store or good bar) are the ones I'm going to define and describe below. But understand that you can travel to any of these rum countries and find local rums that do not match up to these descriptions.

Puerto Rican Rum

The Puerto Rican rums are about the lightest of rums—in body, flavor, and color. In most cases, they are taken from the first distillation of the alcohol—the tops of the distillation—so they are very light in flavor.

Some of these are silver-white in color, and some are light golden. The golden ones are relatively less dry and have a little more depth of flavor than the whites; but they still fall very much into the light and dry rum classification. So the white and gold label rums are generally interchangeable in drink making, depending upon individual preferences. They are right for delicate drinks and light punches.

One Puerto Rican rum, Bacardi Añejo, falls into the medium classification for rum: medium color, body, and flavor.

Cuban Rum

Though they are always having a first-class revolution down there and we are not talking to them at this time, the Cubans still make some of the most popular rums in the world. Sometimes they make their rum from a combination of sugar cane juice and molasses, sometimes just the sugar cane juice. But however they do it, the result is a light rum with a lightly sweet flavor. It is unequaled for mild-flavored cocktails or for highballs with soda or plain water. Not available in the United States at this time.

Jamaica Rum

Jamaica produces both light and dark types of rum. But whether light or dark, these rums carry a rounded pungency that is distinctive. So even a light Jamaica will be much more definite and unique in flavor than its counterpart "light" from another island.

The achievement of this perfumy rum is due, in part, to the continued use of the old pot still. (The continuous still is also used.) And a lot has to do with the yeast culture that is used and the fermentation process.

Because of their outstanding flavor, Jamaica rums are usually used in drinks in combination with milder-flavored rums. And they are favored by candy and pastry makers for flavoring.

In Jamaica, J. Wray and Nephew Group Limited are sort of the smarty-pants people in rum. They produce good stuff. As a matter of fact, they blend Mai Tai rum for Trader Vic.

Virgin Islands Rum

Rums from the Virgin Islands are mostly light or medium light, but they're unaged. And they are really neither fish nor fowl; they can't seem to make up their minds what they are trying to be. Some people like their character. Personally, I don't.

Haitian Rum

The rum from Haiti is made entirely from pressed sugar cane juice, not molasses. It is usually aged longer than rums from other islands. And it turns out to be one of the most pleasing rums of all to me—lush and full of flavor and yet with lots of smooth finesse. It is deep amber in color and medium-bodied. It is simultaneously rich and subtle.

From time to time, somebody makes a nice thing worth talking about. And I am calling your attention to Haitian Rhum Barbancourt. It is the only rum coming out of Haiti to us now. It is just one helluva rum, really a brandy-type rum to be enjoyed in highballs or as a straight liqueur. It is hard to beat.

If you ever want to sip a fine rum after dinner as you would a cognac—and I strongly recommend that you do—pour out a Barbancourt 5-star. You'll never want brandy again. Here's where good aging shows.

Though Barbancourt can stand up to the most severe tasting all on its own and not mixed, it still performs gorgeously in mixed drinks. Make a Trader Vic Daiquiri with a Barbancourt 5-star rum, and you'll have a daiquiri beyond belief.

Even in cooking, the specialness of Barbancourt shows through. Soak a cake in it, and the rum just floats in, and the flavor is soft. Other rums can be too hot or harsh or heavy.

Incidentally, it seems that in Haiti, Barbancourt is so honored that even cookbooks and drink books call for Barbancourt as an ingredient; they don't even say "rum."

Martinique Rum

Martinique rums are similar to dark Jamaica rums because they are dark and pungent in flavor and aroma. They are especially suitable for flavoring sweets and for making rum punches of the heavier variety.

Some of the Martinique rums are distilled and bottled in Martinique for export to us (Rhum St. James); some are distilled in Martinique, shipped to France for aging, and reshipped to us as French rum (Negrita). These French rums are extremely dark and carry more of a molasses taste than the Martinique-bottled rum; the French like them in wintertime hot grogs.

Barbados Rum

Barbados rums are amber-colored and light and clear in flavor. They are sort of a brandy-type rum in their finesse. They are full but light in aroma, not too fruity, not too perfumy, and they are very fine. They are slightly heavier-flavored and -bodied than Cuban and Puerto Rican rums.

Because of their clean flavor, they can be mixed in any type of drink without giving too much flavor. They are very good mixers for all kinds of punches and nice drinks. They are fantastic. You will enjoy them.

Trinidad Rum

We get Siegert's Bouquet from Trinidad. The same people who make the rum make Angostura bitters. They distill a nice little rum, very mild. It is rich amber in color, medium-bodied and -flavored, soft and mellow apple-butterscotchy in aroma and taste. Cocktails and punches made with Siegert's are very good. It is perfect for the Ocean View Rum Punch.

Fernandes rums from Trinidad are also good.

Guyana Rums

The nicest rums from Guyana, South America, are known as the Demeraras (they are named for the county in which they are distilled). They are similar to dark Jamaicas in their aromatic and pungent flavors, but I also find in them a slight dry burnt sugar flavor. The rums bottled in Guyana for export to us are medium-dark, and they are great rums for making punches or in drinks, such as old-fashioneds, where you want a full-flavored rum. Demerara rums bottled in Great Britain generally are dark, and they are especially good for hot drinks. Some Guyana rums go up to 160 proof.

Mexican Rum

Mexico generally distills light-bodied, mildly flavored rums. The most popular are golden in color.

Some of the large Puerto Rican rum companies now have distilleries in Mexico where they produce light-bodied Puerto Rican-type rums.

Hawaiian Rum

A guy has to put something in about Hawaiian rum if he's writing a book on rums. The rum made in Hawaii is a very light rum. It tastes like the inside of a Greek wrestler's hatband, and it is just about as popular in the Islands. I don't know: Someday maybe somebody is going to make a good rum in the Islands; they produce enough sugar cane for it. But what they make now misses the boat for some reason or other.

Philippine Rum

It is a little difficult to get Philippine rum nowadays. But it used to be a fine rum. The distillation is light, similar to that of Puerto Rico. But the flavor is distinctive, faintly reminiscent of vanilla beans.

Philippine rum makes the finest rum and Coca-Cola (Cuba Libre) in the world. And it makes a helluva daiquiri.

New England Rum

At one time, there were a half-dozen New England rums of note, and now they have dwindled down to three. New England rum started out way back in the days when there was a brisk trade on New England-manufactured goods shipped down to the Caribbean. Then the islands had nothing to return but sugar and molasses. The seamen on board these trade ships started to make rum and drink it along the way. Eventually, the stuff came to be distilled in New England. Later on it became part of the triangular trade among Africa, the islands of the West Indies, and New England: New England sent rum to Africa; Africa sent slaves to the West Indies; and the West Indies sent molasses to New England to be made into more rum.

New England rum today is usually deep amber, sort of a brandy-type rum. But really, it is a New England rum, and it is all by its little old self, not like anything else. And it's also good.

Trader Vic's Mai Tai Rum

Now, you know, I shouldn't write about my own stuff. But I am only going to write about one of my rums, so the competitors shouldn't get too mad.

We originated the drink called the Mai Tai. It called for 2 ounces of seventeen-year-old J. Wray and Nephew rum. In a matter of two years after we launched the drink, we had used up all of the seventeen-year-old J. Wray in the world. So I took a bottle of the seventeen-year-old as a standard and blended other rums to try to match it. I took light West Indies, high-ester Jamaica, and a little Martinique and put them all together. My blend never tasted exactly the same as the seventeen-year-old, because that original stuff was hard to beat. But my blend came awfully close. And that is what our Trader Vic Mai Tai rum is today—just one helluva rum for rum punches and cocktails such as old-fashioneds.

About Rum Duties

Let me clarify this to you, kids, about duty on rum and why you have to pay so much for some rums—and why you can't even buy some of the best rums of the world.

We live in a country that likes to do things for other people—in the form of grants or gifts, ways that make the government look big and powerful and generous. But when it comes right down to the nitty-gritty, we really nail some of the developing countries to the cross. I am talking about just one thing: rum.

If you are interested, see how much duty an importer here has to pay on a case of rum from such places as Trinidad and Haiti compared with the duty-free rums from the United States commonwealth and trust territories.

Some of the most outstanding rums in the world come from such places as Guyana, Martinique, Trinidad, Haiti, Barbados, Jamaica, the Philippines, Colombia, Brazil, Africa. But due to the duty and trade restrictions, they can't come into our country in any quantity.

It is about time that we got honest with some of our neighbors who are trying to emerge as good independent countries, and allow them to do business with us. Letting rums from our own islands come into our country nearly duty-free and then socking it to these other countries is just not fair.

When it comes down to it: Why don't we practice what we preach?

COOKING WiTH RUM

YO-HO-HO

Here you'll find the best of the rum recipes gathered from throughout the rum islands and my own favorite rum recipes. They range from soups and first courses through fish and desserts.

When I was asked by Doubleday to write this story of rums, I knew the rums and the rum drinks. But I wanted some more information about rum recipes, right from the West Indies rum islands. So I asked Shirley Sarvis, a good friend of mine, to take the trip and really research out the food recipes from the Caribbean. Food writing is Shirley's whole life's work, and she is knowledgeable as hell and just a grand gal. So she went in every nook and cranny of the Caribbean—to every island starting with Jamaica all the way down to Guyana, just about the whole ball of wax—to find out how they cook with rum in the rum islands.

So the island recipes in this book come directly from the people and the cooks at the point of origin. I haven't taken them from every recipe pamphlet you might run across, I haven't copied; and I doubt if some of these have even been in print before. Some of these recipes were overly complicated as I found them, and I have simplified them.

Some of the recipes are not teaspoon-by-teaspoon specific. But it has been my judgment, after reading recipes and cooking over the years, that if you cook all your life by just following what it says in the recipes, you are never going to be a good cook.

So if you come upon a recipe that says to take a dash of this and a little of that, do just that: Take a couple dashes of this and a little of that until you get a flavor that *you* like. Be free to change a measurement: Start your cooking with the basic thoughts in the book and follow through with what tastes good to you.

I'll tell you a little story about my beginning-cooking at a resort where I worked a thousand years ago. We had eighty-five guests there, and I was supposed to make hot cakes for them all. My boss told me to take some eggs and flour and some baking powder, add a little syrup to sweeten, and some oil. I took everything I was told, stirred it up, threw the hot cakes on the griddle, and they immediately turned black on the bottom and burned to hell. I had put in too much syrup and too much oil. I had really pulled a boo-boo. I had to start adding more eggs and flour to cover up the oil and syrup. So where I started out with three gallons of batter, I ended up with seven gallons. In the meantime, people were pounding on the table for their breakfast. . . .

You will probably do something like this in cooking, too; but don't be ashamed; this is the way to learn.

Just taste as you go; and if it tastes good to you, then you've got something. That is the way, and the only way, that you are going to be a good cook. Improvise and learn to trust your feelings. Now, you go ahead and try.

Rum cookery in the Caribbean runs a broad gamut—from the black mama lady cab driver in St. Croix who throws overproof white rum into bread pudding for her family to the French restaurateur in the elite Petionville section of Port-au-Prince, Haiti, who flames his lobster with rum, and all ranges in between.

In the West Indies rum in cooking is rather an expected thing. It is not out of the ordinary. Rum is rather a staple kitchen ingredient (even though you can run into those who say that they wouldn't honorably cook with rum—they'd drink it!). But cooks will vary in their convictions about rum's best uses. Some say that you can never use rum with fish; the rum is too strong for the fish; they nor their ancestors wouldn't consider baking a nice freshly caught whitefish with a seasoning-sprinkling of rum beforehand. Others tell you to do just that. Some say that you don't mix mango and rum; they say that peaches, bananas, grapefruit, oranges, apples, are all okay, but not mango. And a bartender will refute: Why not? One of his best drinks starts out with rum and mango juice. There are those who only cook with overproof white firewater-type rum; and there are those who designate a special kind of rum for every culinary undertaking: a light gold for flavoring a light custard sauce, a delicate aged white for a fresh peach compote, a dark Jamaica for the finish to a moist baked dark chocolate pudding.

But however vehement their opposing convictions, Caribbean cooks cook with rum with assurance—and flair and discretion and enthusiasm.

Still and all, rum was first (and still is) made and meant for drinking. So rum cookery is not an inexhaustible subject if you're at all discriminating. Since rum was not originally meant to be cooked with, but drunk, it is a happy surprise whenever you discover a cooking use for rum that is as good as a drinking use of rum.

Remember that in cooking with rum you are using rum as a flavoring agent and not as an ingredient. So use just a little. More people spoil food by using too much liquor when they need only a little to point things up. And they let liquor overwhelm the good food they started with. Don't you do it—whether you're cooking with rum just as it is or flaming it first.

You generally flame rum in order to burn off the alcohol. Much of the time you don't want rum as rum: You want the essential flavor of rum without the alcohol. That is much of the reason why rum cooks flame rum; it is not just for the show, delightful though that may be. When you flame rum, the only thing burning is the alcohol in the rum, and you don't usually need that. You don't want to get drunk on a rum-flavored dish.

Rums for Cooking

For cooking purposes, it is not generally necessary to be so specific about types of rum to use as for drink formulas. The subtle shades of difference are usually not so perceptible or crucial when weaving rums with food ingredients as when mingling rum in drinks. And, in cooking, the effects of heat may alter some of rum's subtleties.

Among these recipes, only occasionally is it important that *only* a specific rum be used, and I will tell you that. Otherwise, in most rum cookery, you really need only three kinds of rum: light, medium, and dark. In fact, you can get by with buying only two kinds: a light Puerto Rican and a dark Jamaica rum. Then use a mixture of half of each for medium rum.

Here are a few suggestions—among rums commonly available in the United States—of rums to use in each category.

LIGHT   Don Q Puerto Rican, white or gold label
        Trader Vic's Puerto Rican, light or gold label
        Ronrico Puerto Rican, white or gold label

MEDIUM   Rhum Barbancourt from Haiti, 3-star or 5-star
        Lemon Hart Demerara
        Bacardi Añejo

DARK   See if you can find a high-ester, highly perfumed dark Jamaica rum OR
        Myers's Dark Jamaica
        Rhum St. James from Martinique
        Hudson's Bay Demerara

Thick Coconut Milk

The following recipes often call for thick fresh coconut milk. Make it as follows or use frozen unsweetened coconut milk, thawed.

Pour ¾ cup boiling water over the grated meat of 1 coconut. (To grate fresh shelled and peeled ripe coconut easily, whirl small pieces in a blender.) Stir coconut and press down with a spoon. Allow to stand for 20 minutes. Turn coconut into several thicknesses of cheesecloth to strain; squeeze to extract all liquid. If necessary in order to make 1 cup liquid, add a little more water. Makes 1 cup.

SOUPS

Jamaican Pumpkin Soup

When you serve this soup, pass a crystal shaker or decanter of Barbados Pepper Rum (see Index), a medium rum, or a dark rum and let each guest sprinkle drops of rum into his soup to taste.

1 large onion, chopped
About 1 teaspoon curry powder
⅛ teaspoon ground allspice
3 tablespoons butter
2 cups chicken broth
1 cup canned cooked solid-pack
   pumpkin (or 1 cup cooked
   and puréed fresh pumpkin)

1 clove garlic, peeled
¾ to 1 cup Thick Coconut Milk
  (see Index)
Salt (optional)
Fresh parsley, minced

In a kettle, sauté onion, curry, and allspice in butter until onion is tender. Add broth, pumpkin, and garlic and heat to boiling. Add coconut milk and just heat through. Pour into blender container and whirl until smooth. Add salt if necessary. Reheat over low heat if necessary. Center each serving with a light sprinkling of parsley. Makes 4 cups, about 6 first-course servings.

Caribbean Avocado Soup

1 large ripe avocado, peeled and diced	1½ teaspoons fresh lime juice
¼ green bell pepper, seeded and chopped	1½ teaspoons light Puerto Rican rum
1 green onion with part of green top, chopped	About ¾ teaspoon salt
	1 dash Tabasco
1½ cups milk	About 2 tablespoons heavy cream
	Paprika

Put all ingredients except cream and paprika into blender container and whirl until smooth. Correct seasoning. Cover and chill thoroughly. Pour into small soup pots or bowls. Drizzle a spoonful of cream over top of each serving. Sprinkle with paprika. Makes 3 servings.

Terra Nova Flaming Lobster Bisque

In Kingston, the capital of Jamaica, there is a damn nice little hotel where they do a lobster bisque that is out of this stinkin' world. They flame up a little good quality Jamaica rum just to burn off the alcohol and then stick it in the bisque. At the same time, they stir in heavy cream—not stirring it to mix it all up, but nice and easy so it swirls around and you can taste the fresh cream.

Prepare lobster bisque by your own best recipe. For each serving: At serving time, heat 1 tablespoon dark Jamaica rum, ignite, and ladle, flaming, over bisque. When flames die, add 1 tablespoon thick cream and stir in cream and rum just enough to marble through bisque.

Chilled Rum and Plumpot Barbados

From the Buccaneer, St. Croix. A first-course or a dessert soup. Garnish each serving with a fresh lime slice. If you serve it as a dessert, pour on heavy cream if you wish.

1 large can (1 pound, 14 ounces) purple plums in heavy syrup	½ cup light rum
½ cup fresh lime juice	¼ teaspoon ground cinnamon
	Pinch of salt

Remove pits from plums. Put plums with syrup into blender container with remaining ingredients and whirl until smooth. Chill thoroughly. Stir well before serving in chilled cups. Makes 6 servings.

Cuban Black Bean Soup

This is the authentic Cuban Black Bean Soup from La Zaragozana restaurant in San Juan. To make it into a rum version, add 2 tablespoons dark Jamaica rum before reheating. At serving time, stir in 2 tablespoons more rum. Serve with commercial sour cream to add as a topping along with the marinated onions and rice.

A few hours before serving the rum or the non-rum version: Boil a small portion of rice and marinate the rice and about an equal amount of chopped raw onion in enough Spanish olive oil and vinegar to cloak well. Add 1 soup spoon of this to each serving of the soup.

1 pound black beans
2 quarts water
2 tablespoons salt
5 cloves garlic, peeled
½ tablespoon ground cumin
½ tablespoon crumbled dried
 oregano

2 tablespoons white vinegar
⅔ cup Spanish olive oil
½ pound onions, finely chopped
½ pound green peppers, finely
 chopped

Soak beans in water overnight. Add salt and boil beans until soft. Crush in a mortar the garlic, cumin, and oregano with the vinegar. Heat the oil in a pan, add the onions and peppers, and fry until the onions are golden. Add the crushed ingredients and fry slowly. Drain some of the water off the beans. Add fried ingredients. Cool, cover, and chill overnight. Before serving, reheat very slowly. Makes 6 servings.

*

The Rockefeller plantation at Caneel Bay on the Virgin Island of St. John is quite an institution. Sarvis met the chefs there after dinner one night to talk rum recipes. These fellows, Hans Shädler and Karl Steinger, had worked like hell all day and into the night already, yet they still took the time to sit down and talk and enthuse about rum cookery. Nice guys. Here are some of the things that they talked about.

Chilled Mango Bisque

A first-course soup to sip.

Combine in a chilled blender container 1½ cups mango (or peach) nectar, 1½ cups unsweetened pineapple juice, 2 tablespoons dark Jamaica rum, 1 teaspoon fresh lime juice, and about ⅛ teaspoon freshly ground black pepper. Whirl until frothy. Pour into 4 chilled soup cups or glasses. Float a thin lime slice on top of each. Serve immediately. Makes 4 first-course servings.

FIRST COURSES

Tradewinds Cocktail

For each serving, arrange alternately and slightly overlapping on a bed of shredded lettuce large peeled deveined cooked shrimp and thin arc slices of fresh pineapple. Garnish with lime wedges. Serve with Rum Cocktail Sauce (recipe below).

RUM COCKTAIL SAUCE

Stir together until smooth ¼ cup chili sauce, 1 tablespoon catsup, 1 tablespoon mayonnaise, 2 teaspoons medium rum, 1 teaspoon fresh lime juice, ¼ teaspoon Worcestershire, and a generous dash of Tabasco. Serve with Tradewinds Cocktail (above). Makes about ½ cup.

Virgin Islands Papaya Salad

Combine in a salad bowl 4 cups chilled diced fresh papaya, 2 cups chilled diced fresh pineapple, 1 cup very thinly sliced celery, and 1 small sweet onion (such as Italian red or Spanish) or about 4 green onions, minced. Season to taste with salt, pepper if you wish, and fresh lime juice. Toss to coat lightly with mayonnaise that has been lightly seasoned with medium rum. Serve on crisp lettuce leaves. Makes about 6 servings.

Caneel Bay Salad

To serve as a first course, mound lightly onto lettuce-lined small chilled plates.

To serve as a luncheon salad, present in fresh pineapple shells.

½ pound flaked fresh crab meat
½ pound tiny shelled shrimp
1 cup diced fresh pineapple
1 cup diced fresh mango
¾ cup grated fresh coconut

Sour Cream Rum Dressing
  (recipe below)
Grated fresh nutmeg
Watercress sprigs
Lime wedges

Toss crab, shrimp, pineapple, mango, and coconut lightly with enough dressing to cloak well. Sprinkle lightly with nutmeg. Garnish with watercress and lime wedges. Pass remaining dressing. Makes 6 first-course servings or 4 luncheon salad servings.

SOUR CREAM RUM DRESSING

Stir together until smooth ¾ cup commercial sour cream, 2 tablespoons minced green onions with part of green tops, 2 teaspoons fresh lime juice, 2 teaspoons dark Jamaica rum, ¾ teaspoon dry mustard, about ½ teaspoon salt, about ⅜ teaspoon freshly ground black pepper, and a generous dash of Tabasco. Whip 3 tablespoons heavy cream and fold in. Use in Caneel Bay Salad (above). Makes about 1⅓ cups.

Curried Shrimp Salad, Caneel Bay

1 pound cooked shelled deveined
  medium-sized shrimp
1 cup fresh grapefruit segments
1 cup fresh orange segments
1½ cups cooked rice (grains
  should be separate and not
  sticky)

3 tablespoons finely diced green
  bell pepper
Curry Dressing (recipe below)
Salt
Lettuce
Watercress sprigs

Toss shrimp, grapefruit and orange segments, rice, and green pepper with enough dressing to moisten well. Add salt to taste. Serve on lettuce-lined chilled plates. Garnish with watercress. Pass remaining dressing. Makes 6 luncheon salads.

CURRY DRESSING

Sauté 1½ teaspoons curry powder in 2 teaspoons olive oil until heated through; cool. Beat together with a fork until smooth ⅓ cup commercial sour cream, the curry mixture, 2 teaspoons fresh lime juice, 2 teaspoons medium rum, and ¼ teaspoon salt. Whip 2 tablespoons heavy cream until stiff and fold in. Use in Curried Shrimp Salad, Caneel Bay (above).

Barbados Pepper Rum

Most home cooks still make their own Barbados pepper wine by their own favorite system, even though it appears on Barbados super-market shelves. The supermarket pepper wine is usually dry sherry with various hot peppers in it, with each kind of pepper meant to give its own pepper flavor and hotness to the wine. Since each kind of pep-per has its own character, it is possible to produce vast qualities of pepper wines.

The Bajan Cookbook tells of a rum way to pepper wine, and it is the more likely homemaker's style: Slice 12 to 18 wine peppers and put them into a bottle. Cover with white rum and leave for about a week or 10 days. Then strain and dilute to required "hotness" with good Barbados rum. A few drops of this is a great improvement to any soup.

I like to make Barbados Pepper Rum by soaking black peppercorns in some good Barbados rum. It can be fine when sprinkled into hot soups. Try it in Jamaican Pumpkin Soup (see Index).

Rum Consommé First Course

You can also serve this spooned into avocado half shells, with lime wedges alongside. Or serve it as directed but with lemon wedges alongside instead of lime slices on top.

2 cans (about 10 ounces each) beef consommé	**Minced green-onion tops or snipped chives**
2 tablespoons dark Jamaica rum	**Thin lime slices**

Combine consommé and rum and chill, stirring occasionally, until mixture jells thoroughly, about 8 hours. Spoon into chilled soup pots or cups and top each serving with onions and a lime slice. Makes 6 to 8 servings.

Curried Watermelon First Course

Who the hell ever heard of curried watermelon balls? When I first heard of this, I flipped. When I tasted it, I died. Now, children, try this. It's a helluva first course.

Serve with crisp sesame wafers. Inspired by offerings at Arnos Vale Hotel in Tobago.

Stir together until smooth ½ cup commercial sour cream, about 1½ teaspoons curry powder, ¾ teaspoon salt, a generous dash of Tabasco, 2 teaspoons dark Jamaica rum, and 1 teaspoon fresh lime juice. Just before serving, gently toss with 4 cups cold watermelon balls until evenly cloaked. Spoon into stemmed serving glasses. Garnish each with a mint sprig. Makes 6 servings.

Guyana Golden Cocktail Fruit

Combine equal parts of bite-sized pieces of chilled fresh grapefruit and orange sections (all peel and membrane removed) in individual fruit cocktail glasses set into ice (or other chilled pots or glasses). Top each serving with a generous dash of Angostura bitters and a spoonful of dark rum. Garnish with mint sprigs.

Baked Grapefruit, Bajan Style

From Anthony Sargent, chef at Shady Lane Hotel, Barbados. Serve for breakfast or dessert.

Halve grapefruit. Loosen sections. Sprinkle surfaces of each half with a spoonful each of mild honey, sugar, and medium rum. Dot with butter. Bake in a very hot oven (450°) until bubbly and hot, about 10 minutes. Makes 2 servings.

Grapefruit Tobago

For first course or dessert.

Halve grapefruit. Loosen sections. Sprinkle surfaces of each half with sugar to sweeten, a generous dash of Angostura bitters, and a spoonful of dark or light rum. Dot with butter. Broil slowly until heated through and golden and bubbly on top. Serve hot. Makes 2 servings.

MISCELLANEOUS: HAITIAN OMELET, TRADER VIC'S TORTELLINI, JAMAICAN SPANISH RICE

Haitian Omelet

Cook small pieces of well-smoked lean bacon until almost crisp. Set aside. Sauté thin slices of onion in a small amount of the bacon drippings until tender. Add some very fine dices of fresh green bell peppers and heat through. Add some small dices of seeded fresh tomatoes. Fold into a moist plain Basic Omelet (see Index *except* add a grinding of black pepper). Warm a little (1 to 2 tablespoons for a 2-egg omelet) Barbancourt 3-star rum, ignite, and pour, flaming, over omelet. Spoon flaming liquid over omelet until flames die.

VARIATION: Follow recipe above *except* use sweet onions (such as Italian red or Spanish) instead of regular, use pimientos instead of green bell peppers, and substitute a few moist currants or golden raisins for the tomatoes.

Trader Vic's Tortellini with Cream, Barbados

Make a cream sauce: Melt 1 tablespoon butter in a saucepan. Stir in 1 tablespoon flour to make a paste. Gradually whisk in 1 cup milk. Cook, stirring, to make a smooth sauce. Stir in 3 tablespoons finely diced smoked ham and 1 ounce shredded natural sharp Cheddar cheese. Cook over low heat, stirring, for about 3 minutes. Remove from heat and stir in $\frac{1}{16}$ teaspoon ground nutmeg, $\frac{1}{4}$ teaspoon Worcestershire, and 2 tablespoons Barbados or medium rum. Season with salt and pepper. Cook about 2 dozen tortellini in boiling salted water al dente and drain. Fold into cream sauce. Turn into 2 buttered shallow baking dishes. Sprinkle each serving with 1 tablespoon grated Parmesan cheese. Broil until cheese turns golden. Sprinkle each serving with about 2 tablespoons finely chopped pistachio nuts. Makes 2 servings.

Mrs. dePess's Jamaican Spanish Rice

1 cup uncooked long-grain white
  rice
1½ tablespoons salad oil
6 slices bacon, cut up
1 medium-sized onion, finely
  chopped
3 green onions with part of green
  tops, thinly sliced
½ large green bell pepper, finely
  chopped
1 small can (about 8 ounces)
  tomatoes, drained and
  chopped, or ⅓ cup peeled,
  seeded, and diced fresh
  tomatoes

1 large clove garlic, minced or
  mashed
About ½ teaspoon salt
1 12-ounce bottle (or 1½ cups)
  light beer
1 cup water
2 tablespoons white overproof or
  dark Jamaica rum

In a heavy frying pan over medium heat, sauté rice in oil, stirring, until it is well browned and begins to pop. In a casserole (about 2 quarts), cook bacon slowly until some fat accumulates; add onion, green onions, and green pepper and sauté until limp. Add browned rice along with remaining ingredients except rum; mix thoroughly. Bake uncovered in a moderate oven (350°) for 45 minutes or until rice is just tender. Just before serving, gently stir in rum. Makes 6 servings.

BABS MONTEIL AND SALADS

Woodbrook Cabbage Salad

Handsome young Gordon Siegert, who now heads the Siegert rum and Angostura bitters business and family, knows that he is fortunate to have smiling and kindhearted Babs Monteil for his secretary. Besides being competent in the office, she is an accomplished home cook (creative with rum and bitters), mother, hostess, and wife of one of the most beloved athletes in Port of Spain history (Boisie Monteil).

One of her specialties for a company dinner is a Trinidad pelau of pork, veal, rice, coconut milk, and Angostura bitters. This is the rum-dressed salad to go with the pelau. It is also a good accompaniment for almost any pork, veal, or chicken dish.

3 cups finely shredded cabbage   **Bitters Dressing (recipe below)**
1½ cups finely shredded carrots   **Sliced ripe tomatoes**
¾ cup shredded green bell
  peppers

Toss cabbage, carrots, and peppers with enough dressing to moisten well and yet keep vegetables crisp. Garnish generously with tomatoes. Makes 6 servings.

BITTERS DRESSING

Beat together with a fork until smooth ½ cup mayonnaise, 2 table-spoons olive oil, 1 teaspoon vinegar, 1 teaspoon fresh lime juice, 1 teaspoon Angostura bitters, 4 teaspoons medium rum, ¼ teaspoon Dijon-style mustard, about ⅜ teaspoon salt, about ¼ teaspoon freshly ground black pepper, and 1 clove garlic, minced or mashed. Use as dressing for Woodbrook Cabbage Salad (above). Makes about ¾ cup.

NOTE: This same rum dressing is also good tossed with broken leaves of tender lettuce and some finely shredded green peppers. Squeeze on lime juice if you wish.

Babs Monteil's Chicken Salad

Make chicken salad as usual of diced cooked chicken, chopped celery, sliced green onions, a little chopped parsley, and coarsely chopped walnuts (optional). Season the mayonnaise dressing with a little Dijon-style mustard, a lot of Angostura bitters, a little medium rum, fresh lime juice, salt, and pepper.

Ponche de Crema

Christmas Eve is a good time for this Trinidadian Christmas drink. Also offer nuts or assorted biscuits or cookies.

This recipe is Babs Monteil's own way. Published recipes are not the same. Even those who don't drink much rum love this, says Babs.

Use more condensed milk if you like a sweeter drink. Sprinkle very lightly with grated nutmeg if you wish.

6 eggs

2 cans (15 ounces each) sweetened condensed milk

1 can (13 ounces) evaporated milk

1 cup Old Oak Trinidadian rum (or ½ cup light Puerto Rican rum and ½ cup dark Jamaica rum)

2 generous dashes Angostura bitters

Beat eggs until thick and fluffy. Gradually beat in remaining ingredients in order listed. Chill thoroughly. Stir well before serving. Pour over cracked ice in rather small glasses. Makes 2 quarts.

Avocado-grapefruit Salad

Arrange grapefruit sections (all peel and membrane removed) and peeled ripe avocado slices in a shallow salad platter or on individual lettuce-lined salad plates. Ladle on a rum dressing made in these proportions: Shake or beat together 3 tablespoons light salad oil, 1 tablespoon fresh lemon juice, 1 tablespoon light rum, about ½ teaspoon minced green onion with part of green tops, ½ teaspoon minced fresh parsley, about ⅛ teaspoon dry mustard, and salt and pepper to taste. Add ripe persimmon slices if you wish.

Rum Shrimp-stuffed Avocados

1 large sweet onion (such as Italian red or Spanish) cut (top to bottom) into ⅛-inch-wide wedge slices	Freshly ground black pepper
1 pound tiny shrimp	3 tablespoons dark Jamaica rum
½ cup salad oil	2 or 3 large or 4 small ripe avocados, peeled, halved, and pits removed
4 tablespoons white wine vinegar	Soft lettuce leaves
About 2 tablespoons Dijon-style mustard	Lime wedges

Separate onion wedges into small arcs; combine with shrimp. Beat oil, vinegar, mustard, and a generous grinding of pepper together with an electric mixer or rotary beater until smooth and thickened; pour over shrimp and onions. Cover and chill for 12 to 24 hours; turn occasionally. Fold in rum. Arrange each avocado on a lettuce-lined plate. Spoon shrimp mixture into and over avocado cavities. Garnish each with a lime wedge. Makes 4 to 6 luncheon salads or 8 first-course salads.

Lobster Salad with Rum Dressing

Especially in Jamaica, the cooks talk about spicing the dressing for their lobster salad with rum. They use the salad as a salad or in a sandwich.

Combine dices or slices of cooked lobster meat with thinly sliced celery and dress generously with this dressing: Stir together equal parts mayonnaise and sour cream and a little lemon juice and a little dark Jamaica rum to season. Season salad with salt and pepper. Garnish with hard-cooked egg slices and a fine sprinkling of parsley.

For the best lobster salad sandwich: Make it open-faced. Split nice big fat hot dog buns and hollow out the soft centers to leave a shell. Brush the shells with melted butter and broil quickly until golden and crisp. Immediately line the shells with a little leaf lettuce, fill with the chilled lobster salad, and serve.

FISH AND SHELLFISH

Guyana Prawns

1½ pounds large raw shrimp (about 12 to 15 per pound size)	**4 tablespoons minced shallots**
	3 tablespoons dark rum
Salt	**½ cup heavy (whipping) cream**
Freshly ground black pepper	**½ teaspoon Dijon-style mustard**
⅓ cup butter	**Watercress sprigs**

Shell and devein shrimp; pat dry. Season very generously with salt and lightly with pepper. In a large frying pan over medium-high heat, melt butter until it bubbles. Add shallots and shrimp and sauté just until shrimp are barely pink and opaque throughout, about 3 minutes. Warm rum in a small pan, ignite, and pour over shrimp. Ladle liquid over shrimp until flames die. Beat cream and mustard together until smooth. Add to frying pan. Heat to bubbling and simmer for a few minutes until sauce cooks down slightly. Correct seasoning with salt and pepper. Garnish with watercress. Makes 4 servings.

Rum Lobster Thermidor

Make lobster thermidor by your usual recipe *except* substitute dark Jamaica rum for the sherry or brandy called for.

Rum-broiled Lobster or Shrimp

Broil or charcoal-grill large shelled shrimp or lobster in shell as usual except baste before and during grilling with rum melted butter made in these proportions: 1 tablespoon dark Jamaica rum stirred into ⅓ cup melted butter. Watch carefully so that shellfish does not ignite. Serve with additional rum melted butter as a dipping sauce.

Rum-broiled Shrimp

More specifically for shrimp.

1½ pounds large raw shrimp (about 8 to 15 per pound size)
½ cup melted butter
2 tablespoons dark Jamaica rum
2 large cloves garlic, minced or mashed
3 tablespoons finely chopped fresh parsley

About ¾ teaspoon salt
About ½ teaspoon freshly ground black pepper
About ⅛ teaspoon crushed dried hot red peppers

Shell and devein shrimp, leaving tail shells on. Combine remaining ingredients in a bowl, add shrimp, and allow to stand at room temperature for 1 hour; turn occasionally. Arrange shrimp in marinade well apart in a single layer in a shallow broiling tray. Broil on both sides about 6 inches from heat *just* until shrimp turn pink and lose translucence, about 4 minutes on each side. Serve hot with marinade spooned over. Makes appetizers for about 6 or main course for 3.

Rum Lobster

A baking method for lobster tails. The seasoning ideas come from Chez Guerard, Petionville, Haiti.

4 spiny lobster tails (about 8 ounces each)
¾ cup butter
1½ tablespoons fresh lemon juice

1 tablespoon dark rum
⅜ teaspoon Dijon-style mustard
Grinding of black pepper

Thaw frozen lobster tails. Cut away and remove under shells. Cut away center section of tail. Gently loosen meat from shell but leave it attached at tail. Lift loose meat out of shell groove and place it over back of shell by gently pulling it between remaining tail sections. Slit the thin membrane covering lobster meat down center to prevent curling. Melt butter and stir in lemon juice, rum, mustard, and pepper; brush generously over both sides of lobster meat. Place lobster in a greased shallow pan and bake in a hot oven (450°) for about 10 minutes or just until opaque throughout; baste occasionally with rum butter. Serve with remaining rum butter as a dipping sauce. Makes 4 servings.

Deviled Crab Flambé

The Jamaicans usually say that they use a white overproof rum to spike their deviled crab. Here we use dark Jamaica.

You can add a little spicing rum to your own recipe for deviled crab this way or follow the recipe below: For each serving, add 1½ tablespoons dark Jamaica rum to the crab sauce. Just before serving, pour about 1 tablespoon rum over the dish and flame. The rum adds a smoky, toasty quality.

Make a thick cream sauce using basic proportions of 3 tablespoons butter, 3 tablespoons flour, and 1 cup milk. Sauté 3 to 4 tablespoons finely minced onion in 2 tablespoons butter until very tender. Add 1 cup flaked crab meat and ½ teaspoon dry mustard (more if you like a hotter dish) and turn to mix well. Stir 1½ tablespoons dark Jamaica rum into ¾ cup of the thick cream sauce; fold in crab mixture. Season with salt and pepper. Pile into a buttered shell. Arrange 2 large pieces of crab legs on top. Sprinkle with about 4 teaspoons grated Parmesan cheese and dust lightly with paprika. Pour 1 tablespoon melted butter over top. Bake in a very hot oven (450°) for 5 minutes. To serve: Fill a platter with a bed of rock salt. Place shell-dish of crab on it. Pour 1 to 2 tablespoons dark Jamaica rum over the top. Ignite. Sprinkle lightly with minced parsley. Makes 1 serving.

Rum Fish, Port of Spain

Serve with fresh lime wedges to garnish.

2 pounds fillets of red snapper (or other rockfish)
⅓ cup salad oil
¼ cup light rum
1 tablespoon fresh lime juice
2 tablespoons minced green onions with part of green tops
2 tablespoons minced green bell peppers
1 large clove garlic, minced or mashed

¾ teaspoon salt
⅜ teaspoon crumbled dried thyme
About ¼ teaspoon crushed dried hot red peppers (more if you want a hotter sauce)
¼ teaspoon freshly ground black pepper
⅛ teaspoon sugar

Wipe fish dry with a damp cloth. Arrange close together in a single layer in an oiled shallow baking dish. Stir together remaining ingredients with a fork to mix well. Spoon over fish. Cover and chill for 2 hours. Bake in a moderate oven (350°) just until thickest part flakes with a fork, about 20 minutes. Serve with baking juices spooned over. Makes 4 servings.

Rum-broiled Fish

From Montegonian, Owner Mickey, Montego Bay.

Brush fish fillets or steaks to be broiled very generously with melted butter. Season with salt and pepper. Sprinkle with a very little Worcestershire. Squeeze on a little fresh lime or lemon juice to season. Sprinkle lightly with dark Jamaica rum. Broil.

Ocean View Fish Pie

For serving in his hotel restaurant, Hamish Gordon compiles this dish in layers, tops it with mashed potatoes, bakes it, and serves it as a fish pie. For home cooking, we do it more simply in a single layer. His fish would be flying fish, dolphin, or kingfish. We can use red snapper or cod or other rockfish.

Good accompaniments are fresh corn on the cob, parsleyed rice, and cold beer or a dry California Sauvingnon Blanc or Dry Semillon.

2 pounds fillets of red snapper (or cod or other rockfish)
6 tablespoons olive oil
¼ cup medium rum
2 tablespoons sweet sherry
1 tablespoon fresh lime juice
4 tablespoons chopped peeled and seeded tomatoes (fresh or canned)
3 tablespoons minced green onions with part of green tops
2 tablespoons minced green bell peppers
4 tablespoons moist seedless golden raisins
4 tablespoons chopped stuffed green olives
1 tablespoon capers
1 large clove garlic, minced or mashed
¾ teaspoon salt
¾ teaspoon ground ginger
½ teaspoon ground nutmeg
¼ teaspoon freshly ground black pepper
⅛ teaspoon sugar
3 tablespoons grated Parmesan cheese
Lime wedges

Wipe fish dry with a damp cloth. Arrange close together in a single layer in an oiled shallow baking dish. Stir together remaining ingredients except Parmesan and lime wedges to mix well. Spoon evenly over fish. Sprinkle with Parmesan. Bake in a moderate oven (350°) just until thickest part of fish flakes with a fork, about 25 minutes. Serve with baking juices spooned over. Garnish with lime. Makes 4 servings.

CHICKEN AND MONSIEUR GARDÈRE

Poulet en Rhum Gelée, Haitienne

Poulet en rhum gelée. That's fancy as hell. It means chicken in aspic. But this is the best thing you ever put into your little *bouche.*

Serve this as a luncheon or supper salad. Use any olive oil remaining from the chicken cooking to make into an oil-vinegar dressing for an accompanying green lettuce salad.

¼ cup olive oil
2 large frying chicken breasts, split and boned (4 breast pieces)
Salt
1 cup thinly sliced leeks
3 carrots, peeled and thinly sliced crosswise
1 small can or jar (2 ounces) pimientos, drained and coarsely chopped

About 15 whole black peppercorns
1 can (13 ounces) clear consommé madrilène
2 tablespoons medium rum
Lettuce leaves
1 ripe avocado, peeled and thinly sliced
Orange Mayonnaise (recipe below)

Pour olive oil over bottom of a heavy shallow casserole. Season chicken with salt and arrange in casserole in a single layer, skin side down. Sprinkle with half of the leeks, half of the carrots, half of the pimientos, and half of the peppercorns. Sprinkle with additional salt to season. Top with remaining leeks, carrots, pimientos, peppercorns, and salt to season. Heat madrilène to melt; remove from heat and stir in rum; pour evenly over casserole contents. Cover casserole and simmer for 1½ hours or until chicken is very tender. Remove from heat, allow to cool at room temperature, then chill overnight. Next day, being careful not to disturb casserole layering, pour off any excess olive oil. Return casserole to refrigerator for 1 hour or more. At serving time, unmold chicken onto a chilled serving platter (invert casserole over platter). Garnish with lettuce leaves and avocado slices. Pass mayonnaise. Makes 4 servings.

ORANGE MAYONNAISE

Stir together until smooth ½ cup mayonnaise, ¼ cup commercial sour cream, 1½ teaspoons grated fresh orange peel, 1 teaspoon dry mustard, 1 teaspoon fresh lemon juice, ½ teaspoon crumbled dried thyme, and ¼ teaspoon crumbled dried oregano. Let stand for 30 minutes or more. Serve with Poulet en Rhum Gelée, Haitienne (above). Makes about ¾ cup.

Barbados Barbecued Chicken

This simple marinating treatment makes chicken unusually chicken-flavorful and tender. You won't taste rum, just subtly seasoned better chicken. From Anthony Sargent, chef at Shady Lane Hotel, Barbados.

Turn chicken pieces to be barbecued in a mixture of enough light rum to cloak very generously, a very generous grating of fresh ginger, split cloves of garlic (optional), and salt and pepper to season well. Cover and chill for 24 hours; turn occasionally. Drain and grill over charcoal as usual, brushing with melted butter.

Rum Almond Chicken

About 4 whole large chicken breasts, split, boned, and skinned (2 pounds of boned meat)
Salt
Freshly ground black pepper
½ cup butter
3 cans (6 ounces each) frozen orange juice concentrate, thawed
6 tablespoons medium rum
¾ cup lightly toasted slivered almonds
Watercress sprigs

Cut each breast piece diagonally into five pieces. Season generously with salt and pepper. Heat butter in a large frying pan over medium heat until it bubbles. Add chicken and sauté just until meat loses translucency and is tender, about 12 minutes total. With a slotted spoon, remove chicken and arrange over bottom of a shallow casserole (about 1½ to 2 quarts). Add to butter in frying pan the juice concentrate, 1 teaspoon salt, and ½ teaspoon pepper. Cook over high heat, stirring, until sauce blends and browns slightly and is reduced by nearly half. Stir in rum. Pour sauce over chicken. Bake uncovered in a moderate oven (350°) until heated through and bubbling, about 20 minutes. Sprinkle with almonds and bake for 5 minutes more. Garnish generously with watercress. Makes 6 servings.

Miss Chin-Sue's Chicken

½ cup soy sauce
¼ cup light Puerto Rican rum
⅓ cup chopped onion
1 tablespoon finely grated fresh
   ginger
1 clove garlic, minced or mashed
3-pound frying chicken, cut into
   serving pieces

4 tablespoons melted butter
3 tablespoons catsup
1 teaspoon sugar
1 teaspoon vinegar
⅛ teaspoon monosodium
   glutamate
⅛ teaspoon freshly ground black
   pepper

Stir together soy sauce, rum, onion, ginger, and garlic. Add chicken pieces, turn to coat well, cover, and chill for 6 hours; turn occasionally. Drain chicken and arrange in a single layer in a buttered shallow baking pan. Stir together remaining ingredients and brush over chicken. Bake in a slow oven (325°) for 1 hour or until chicken is tender; turn once. Makes 4 servings.

Chicken Barbancourt

The way Sarvis got this recipe is worth talking about: She was nosing around Haitian restaurants and went up to the manager of the El Rancho in Petionville and asked if she could talk to the chef. The request was granted. And the chef turned out to be this nice little Haitian guy, Chef Dureau. He said he had a recipe called Chicken Barbancourt that he cooks. He tried to tell how to make it, but quickly gave up with the limitations of the language. So he told Sarvis to come early for lunch that day and he would cook the chicken for her and she could watch how.

2½-pound frying chicken, cut
   into serving pieces
3 green onions with part of green
   tops, coarsely cut
2 tablespoons fresh parsley leaves

⅛ teaspoon crushed dried hot
   red peppers
½ cup fresh orange juice
6 tablespoons Barbancourt rum
¼ cup fresh lime juice

4 large cloves garlic, peeled	Flour
1 teaspoon crumbled dried thyme	About 3 tablespoons butter
1 teaspoon salt	Peeled thin orange slices
¼ teaspoon freshly ground black pepper	Fresh parsley, minced
	Sliced almonds, lightly toasted

Rinse chicken and dry well. Combine next 10 ingredients in a blender and whirl until smooth. Pour blended mixture over chicken and allow to marinate for 1 hour. Drain chicken, saving marinade; squeeze chicken and wipe dry; dust lightly with flour. In a heavy frying pan over medium heat, brown chicken pieces well on all sides in butter. Add reserved marinade, cover, and simmer until chicken is tender, turning once, about 30 minutes. Remove chicken to serving platter. Cook and stir juices in pan to blend and cook down slightly. Pour over chicken. Garnish with oranges. Sprinkle lightly with parsley and almonds. Makes 4 servings.

Haitian Coconut-crusted Rum Chicken

6 whole frying chicken breasts, split and boned (12 breast pieces)	About ¼ teaspoon powdered saffron
Salt	1 large jar (4 ounces) sliced pimientos
Freshly ground black pepper	4 tablespoons dried currants
About 5 tablespoons butter	2 tablespoons Barbancourt or dark Jamaica rum
2 large sweet onions (such as Italian red or Spanish), very thinly sliced	1 tablespoon fresh lemon juice
4 teaspoons brown sugar	Coconut Crust (recipe below)

Season chicken pieces generously with salt and pepper. Fold loose corners of each breast piece under to form a compact triangle of meat. In a frying pan, gently brown chicken pieces on all sides in about 4 tablespoons of the butter. Arrange in a single layer in a shallow baking dish. Add 1 tablespoon butter to drippings in frying pan. Add onions and sauté until tender. Stir in brown sugar, ½ teaspoon salt, saffron, pimientos, currants, rum, and lemon juice. Spoon evenly over chicken. Cover and bake in a moderate oven (375°) for 45 minutes or until chicken is tender. Remove cover and sprinkle Coconut Crust over chicken. Return to oven and bake uncovered until coconut toasts lightly, about 10 minutes. Spoon juices over chicken as you serve. Makes 6 generous servings.

COCONUT CRUST

Toss together thoroughly 5 tablespoons melted butter, 2 table-spoons Barbancourt or dark Jamaica rum, 1 tablespoon fresh lemon juice, ½ teaspoon salt, ½ teaspoon freshly ground black pepper, 2 cups flaked coconut, and 4 tablespoons chopped fresh parsley. Use with Haitian Coconut-crusted Rum Chicken (above).

More! Chicken

My chef was talking about rum in my office the other day and said, "You know, we cooked a dish at home with morels and a little rum and chicken, and it was awfully good; it's entirely different."

The recipe calls for dried morel mushrooms. They are just about as hard to find as gold nuggets, but they taste a lot better.

2 whole frying chicken breasts, boned
Salt
Freshly ground black pepper
Flour
About 3 tablespoons butter
1 tablespoon minced green onions (white part only)
1¼ cups chicken broth
½ cup sliced cooked artichoke bottoms
2 tablespoons dried morels, soaked until soft and sliced
2 tablespoons heavy (whipping) cream
3 tablespoons medium rum
1 teaspoon fresh lemon juice

Wipe chicken dry, season with salt and pepper, and dust lightly with flour. In a large frying pan over medium heat, brown breasts on both sides in butter. Remove chicken. Add onion to pan and sauté until coated with butter. Add 1½ tablespoons flour and stir to make a paste. Gradually add chicken broth and cook and stir to make a smooth sauce. Return chicken to pan, add artichokes and morels, and spoon sauce over. Cover and simmer for 20 minutes or until breasts are tender. Stir in cream, rum, and lemon juice and just heat through. Correct seasoning with salt and pepper. Makes 2 servings.

Chicken Jamaican

3 whole large chicken breasts, split, boned, and skinned if you wish (6 breast pieces; if you like a good deal of sauce, use only 4)
Salt
Freshly ground black pepper
4 tablespoons butter
1 large can (12 ounces) frozen orange juice concentrate, thawed
1 large bay leaf, finely crumbled
3 tablespoons creamy peanut butter
3 tablespoons dark Jamaica rum
1 tablespoon fresh lime juice
1 ripe but firm banana, thinly sliced
Finely chopped roasted peanuts
Guava jelly, cut into small cubes

Season chicken generously with salt and pepper. Fold loose corners of each piece under to form a compact piece of meat. In a heavy frying pan over medium heat, brown breasts on both sides in butter. Reduce heat to low. Add orange juice concentrate, bay, about ½ teaspoon salt, and ¼ teaspoon pepper. Cover and simmer until chicken is tender, about 15 minutes. With slotted spoon, remove chicken pieces to warm serving plates; keep warm. Add peanut butter to juices in frying pan and whisk until blended. Stir in rum and lime juice. Add banana slices and just heat through. Pour sauce over chicken. Sprinkle with peanuts. Garnish with jelly. Makes 6 servings (4 if only 4 breast pieces are used).

Here is a nice story about how nice people can be.

When Shirley Sarvis was in Haiti to help me write this book, she met Louis Gardère of the Barbancourt rum family. (Of course, I had written to Mr. Gardère beforehand.) Not only did he receive Sarvis in the most gracious way, but he presented her with rum recipes that he had already gathered for us. Two of those recipes, Poulet en Cocotte Barbancourt and Soufflé au Chocolat, are very special to us because Mr. Gardère had written to his daughter in Paris to get them.

Poulet en Cocotte Barbancourt (Chicken in Stewpan Barbancourt)

Sauté a cut-up chicken, salted and peppered, in 2 tablespoons of butter. Remove the chicken when it has browned and sauté in the butter 1 thumb-cube of bacon (more or less), cut up. Add:

1 large onion, chopped	**3 cubes bouillon (optional)**
1 cup water	**1 small box (6 ounces)**
1 cup rum	**mushrooms**

Place chicken back in pan. Add some very small potatoes (new potatoes) or 2 medium-sized potatoes, cut up. Cover the casserole and allow it to cook, adding water if necessary and thyme, pepper, salt, and garlic.

Soufflé au Chocolat

If the translation from French leaves a little to be wondered upon, so it also gives a moderate culinary challenge.

⅓ cup butter	**3 ounces bitter chocolate (or**
⅓ cup sifted flour	**equivalent in cocoa)**
⅓ teaspoon salt	**4 egg yolks and 5 whites**
⅓ teaspoon cream of tartar	**¾ cup sugar**
Bitter of orange	**9 ounces milk**

Grate chocolate; mix in double boiler with butter. Add flour, milk, and salt until thickened. Remove from heat. Beat the 4 egg yolks and add the sugar and bitter of orange, then blend the two mixtures. To this, add the 5 egg whites, beaten stiff with cream of tartar. Pour onto a deep plate of enameled metal (if possible) and place it in a plate of very hot water. Heat at 350° for 45 to 55 minutes. Meanwhile, prepare a sauce as follows: In an earthenware pot set in a plate of hot water make a paste of ¾ cup butter and 1½ cups powdered sugar and add 1 or 2 eggs beaten with ⅓ cup rum. Serve hot with the soufflé, which you flame at the table with ⅓ to ¾ cup of warm rum (for this operation, Barbancourt 3-star does very well). Makes 9 servings.

*

Monsieur Gardère didn't stop there. He also arranged for Sarvis to meet Mrs. Faubert, a lovely Petionville widow and fine hostess. One afternoon in her home, Mrs. Faubert told of some of her rum cooking favorites. She knows what she's talking about.

Rum Raisin Sauce, Haiti

Mrs. Faubert makes this rum sauce to ladle over plain sponge cake or her baked sweet potato pudding or butter cake, pound cake, *baba au rhum,* or bananas baked with brown sugar and butter.

Soak ½ cup moist seedless raisins in ½ cup pungent golden rum, such as Barbancourt 3-star, for 2 hours. In a saucepan, heat 1 cup water and ⅓ cup sugar to boiling, then simmer for 15 minutes. Add 2 tablespoons guava jelly and melt. Drain raisins, saving rum. Add raisins to saucepan and simmer until plump, about 15 minutes. Remove from heat and stir in reserved rum and 1 teaspoon fresh lemon juice. Makes over 1 cup.

Though delicious, this is a vividly sweet sauce, so we like to cut it with custard sauce and sponge cake. It makes for a double saucing and a very lavish dessert: Ladle warm raisin sauce over thin slices of plain sponge cake. Top with a ladling of soft custard sauce (follow recipe for Soft Custard Rum Sauce [see Index] *except* omit rum and increase vanilla to 1½ teaspoons) and sprinkle very lightly with nutmeg.

Mrs. Faubert's Haitian Fruit Cup

3 cups melon balls cut from any fresh melon (or mixed melons) such as watermelon, honeydew, Crenshaw, cantaloupe, Persian, casaba

Sections cut from 1 large grapefruit

Sections cut from 2 oranges

2 large nectarines or peaches, peeled and sliced

⅓ to ½ cup firmly packed light brown sugar

⅓ cup Barbancourt 3-star rum

3 tablespoons fresh orange juice

1 tablespoon grenadine

1 ripe banana, sliced

Fresh mint sprigs

Gently combine all ingredients except banana and mint in an attractive serving bowl. Chill for 4 hours. At serving time, add banana and gently turn to mix. Garnish with mint. Makes 8 servings.

VEAL, PORK, LAMB, AND BEEF

Eggplant-stuffed Veal, Calabash Sue

Garnish with ripe tomato wedges and slender lemon wedges.

1 veal breast (about 3 pounds)   **Freshly ground black pepper**
    with pocket for stuffing   **Eggplant Stuffing (recipe below)**
½ cup light Puerto Rican rum   **6 strips bacon**
Salt

Place veal in a shallow bowl. Add rum and rub over veal surfaces. Cover and chill for 24 hours, turning veal occasionally. Pour off rum. Wipe veal dry and sprinkle surfaces with salt and pepper. Spoon Eggplant Stuffing lightly into veal pocket; close with small skewers. Place in a shallow roasting pan, bone side down. Arrange bacon over top. Bake in a slow oven (300°) for 2 hours. Allow to stand for 15 minutes. Carve into slices, cutting between bones. Makes 4 servings.

EGGPLANT STUFFING

Peel and dice ⅔ pound eggplant. Drop into boiling salted water and cook until tender; drain well. Thoroughly mix with 2 tablespoons fine soft bread crumbs; ⅓ pound ground chuck; ⅓ pound fresh Italian garlic pork sausages (or other well-seasoned pork sausage), cut from casings and crumbled; ¼ cup minced fresh onions; ¼ cup minced fresh parsley; 3 tablespoons finely diced celery; 2 tablespoons finely chopped green bell peppers; 1 slightly beaten egg; about ½ teaspoon salt; ½ teaspoon crumbled dried sweet basil; ¼ teaspoon crumbled dried thyme; ⅛ teaspoon freshly ground black pepper; and 1 large clove garlic, minced or mashed. Use for Eggplant-stuffed Veal, Calabash Sue (above).

Hawaiian Pork Chops

¼ cup soft butter
About 1½ teaspoons salt
2 teaspoons dry mustard
1 teaspoon ground ginger
½ teaspoon freshly ground black
  pepper
4 double-thick pork chops, each
  about 2 inches thick, well
  trimmed

2 cups finely chopped onion
⅔ cup light rum
½ cup finely chopped fresh
  pineapple (or drained canned
  crushed pineapple)
Watercress sprigs

Stir together the butter, salt, mustard, ginger, and pepper to form a paste; rub over surfaces of chops. In a heavy frying pan over medium heat, brown chops well on both sides; remove chops. Add onion to frying pan and sauté until well browned. Return chops to pan, top with onions, and add rum. Cover tightly and bake in a slow oven (325°) until meat is very tender, about 1½ hours (if necessary to keep chops moist, add a little more rum). Lift chops to warm serving platter or plates. Stir pineapple into juices and onions in pan and heat through; spoon over chops. Garnish generously with watercress. Makes 4 servings.

Rum-glazed Spareribs

1 side pork spareribs (about 3
  pounds), cracked in half
  lengthwise and to separate
  end ribs
Salt
Freshly ground black pepper
1 can (8 ounces) tomato sauce

½ cup dark Jamaica rum
½ cup honey
2 tablespoons wine vinegar
3 tablespoons grated or minced
  fresh onion
1 clove garlic, minced or mashed
½ teaspoon Worcestershire

Sprinkle spareribs generously on both sides with salt and pepper. Place in a shallow roasting pan and bake in a hot oven (400°) for 45 minutes. Drain off accumulated fat. Mix together remaining ingredients and pour over spareribs. Reduce oven temperature to 350° and bake ribs for 40 minutes more or until tender. Turn once and baste occasionally during baking. Cut into serving-size pieces. Makes 3 to 4 servings.

Rum Roasted Pork

3- to 5-pound boneless pork loin roast	**Dried thyme, crumbled**
Salt	**Garlic cloves, peeled and slivered**
Coarsely ground black pepper	**Dark Jamaica rum**

With a sharp knife, pierce surface of pork about 1½ inches deep in 6 to 10 places. With forefinger, press into each hole about ¹⁄₁₆ teaspoon *each* salt, pepper, and thyme, and about ¼ clove garlic. Rub surface of roast with enough rum to moisten and with salt, pepper, and thyme. Place pork in a shallow pan. Pour over 6 to 10 tablespoons more rum. Cover and chill for 12 to 24 hours. Turn occasionally. Place on rack in roasting pan and bake in a slow oven (325°), allowing about 40 minutes per pound or until meat thermometer registers about 185°. Allow to stand for about 15 minutes. Meantime, remove from roasting pan all fat and any burned drippings; leave crusty brown drippings. Add ⅔ cup water and 2 tablespoons rum, stir to loosen drippings, and cook and stir over high heat just to blend. Carve pork into thin slices. Pass rum sauce to ladle over. Makes 6 to 10 servings.

Ham Steak with Rum Glaze

2-inch-thick fully cooked smoked ham steak, about 3 pounds	**1 can (1 pound) whole or half apricots**
Whole cloves	**2 tablespoons honey**
½ cup light rum	**2 tablespoons dark Jamaica rum**
Water	**1 teaspoon dry mustard**

Wipe ham dry with a damp cloth. Diagonally slash fat about every 2 inches; insert about 3 cloves in each slash. Place ham in a shallow casserole. Add the light rum and enough water to reach about ½ inch up ham. Cover and bake in a moderate oven (375°) for 45 minutes to 1 hour. Drain syrup from apricots into a saucepan. Boil until reduced to about ⅓ cup. Stir in honey, the dark rum, and mustard. Drain baking juices off ham and discard. Arrange apricots decoratively over top and alongside ham; center each with a clove. Spoon syrup mixture over all. Bake uncovered for 15 minutes more or until glazed; baste once or twice. Carve and serve slices with pan juices and apricots. Makes 6 to 8 servings.

Rum Sausages

In a heavy frying pan, slowly cook fresh Italian link sausages until well browned on all sides and cooked through. Discard any excess fat. Add butter (1 teaspoon per serving) and melt. Add dark rum (1 tablespoon per serving) at edge of pan. Warm rum, ignite, and spoon, flaming, over sausages until flames die. Serve sausages with juices spooned over and a fine sprinkling of minced fresh parsley.

Walter's Rum Sausages

My food director thought this up one morning at ten o'clock. We all tried it and thought it was great.

In a frying pan, brown fresh pork sausage patties in their own fat. Drain off excess fat. Add a little butter. Stir in some chopped shallots and stir to heat through. Add a little medium rum (½ ounce per serving) at edge of the frying pan, heat to warm, ignite, and spoon over sausages until flames die. Add a little brown sauce and broth to moisten sausages. Sprinkle lightly with snipped fresh chives. Cover and simmer until sausages are cooked through.

Cassoulet Haitien

In the mountains out of Port-au-Prince where it is way up high and nice and cool and very beautiful, there is a hotel called the El Rancho. Sometimes on the luncheon menu there is Cassoulet Haitien. I suggest you try it.

Make a French cassoulet as usual *except* add 2 or 3 tablespoons Barbancourt rum before baking.

Trader Vic's Lamb Curry

Curried goat is a special Jamaican dish. It is very much like a good lamb curry and often has coconut milk in it. Sometimes the Jamaican cooks finish a curry off with a little rum accent. My recipe for lamb curry is a good starting point.

Serve with rice. Good accompaniment condiments are fried banana or plantain slices and cooked fresh chard or spinach greens.

¼ cup salad oil

2 tablespoons ground coriander

1 tablespoon ground turmeric

1 teaspoon ground cumin

1 teaspoon freshly ground black pepper

2 pounds boneless leg of lamb, cut into about 1-inch cubes

2 large onions, finely chopped

½ cup butter

2 teaspoons minced fresh ginger

About 2 tablespoons minced fresh hot chili peppers (to taste)

4 cups chicken broth

2 cloves garlic, minced or mashed

1 cup Thick Coconut Milk (see Index)

Salt

1 to 2 tablespoons dark Jamaica rum

Stir together oil, coriander, turmeric, cumin, and black pepper. Add meat and turn to mix thoroughly. Let stand for about 20 minutes. In a heavy kettle, sauté onions in butter until limp. Stir in ginger and chili peppers; push onion mixture to side of kettle. Add meat cubes with marinating mixture and sauté, turning to cook all sides, over low heat. Stir in broth and garlic. Cover and simmer until meat is tender, about 1 hour. Ten minutes before serving, stir in coconut milk. Add salt to taste. Just before serving, stir in rum. Makes 4 to 6 servings.

Flaming Brochettes

You can go around the world and see flaming dishes made with all kinds of stuff. I once even saw a fellow take some plain alcohol to flame a skewerful of beef cubes. But when you go down to Jamaica, it is a cinch that they are not going to use cognac or brandy or any other usual high-proof alcohol. They are going to use rum. And it's not bad; it can taste awfully good. That is what they do at the Montegonian in Montego Bay. Here is one way you can do it.

Marinate cubes of tender beef for broiling for a few hours in light rum and a generous grating of fresh ginger. Dry meat well and thread on skewers along with pieces of vegetables of your choice, such as bell peppers, onions, and tomatoes. Grill brochette over charcoal as usual, basting occasionally with salad oil or melted butter. Season with salt and pepper. At serving time, warm a small amount of light Puerto Rican rum. Ignite and pour, flaming, over brochette. Ladle flaming rum over brochette until flames die.

Rum Steaks Sauté

You will notice that there are few beef recipes in this collection. Beef and rum aren't usually outstandingly compatible. But here is one that is nice.

This, as written, is mellow and refined. For a sauce with higher spicing, follow the same recipe *except* use dark Jamaica rum instead of medium and mix 1 teaspoon Dijon-style mustard into the ⅓ cup soft butter added at the finish.

4 small boneless broiling steaks (such as filets mignon, boneless club, Delmonico), each cut 1 inch thick and about ½ pound, well trimmed	Salt
	Freshly ground black pepper
	4 tablespoons minced shallots
	4 tablespoons medium rum
1½ tablespoons olive oil	⅓ cup soft butter
3 tablespoons butter	2 tablespoons minced fresh parsley

Make small cuts through any gristle edges of each steak to prevent curling. Wipe steaks dry. Heat oil and 1½ tablespoons of the butter in a heavy large frying pan over medium-high heat until butter foams, then begins to stop foaming. Add steaks and sauté until browned on both sides and done to your liking; turn only once (sauté about 5 minutes total for rare). (If necessary, make a small cut in steak to check doneness.) Remove to warm serving plates or platter; season with salt and pepper; keep warm. Remove excess fat from frying pan. Add 1½ tablespoons butter and melt it. Add shallots and sauté just to cloak with butter. Remove from heat. Add rum at edge of pan. When it is warm, ignite it. When flames die, stir in the soft butter, about a tablespoon at a time (keep butter at a thick creamy consistency; do not let it melt down to a thin liquid). Season sauce with salt and pepper. Stir in parsley. Spoon over hot steaks. Makes 4 servings.

THREE VEGETABLES AND A BREAD

Rum Buttered Corn on the Cob

Stir enough (a little) dark Jamaica rum into warm melted butter to season. Pass with a soft brush. Let each eater brush butter over hot ear of cooked corn. Sprinkle with coarse salt to taste.

Whipped or Baked Sweet Potatoes or Yams

Prepare potatoes for whipping or baking as usual. For whipped potatoes: Add dark Jamaica rum to season along with the butter as you whip. For baked potatoes: Arrange cooked sliced potatoes in baking dish and sprinkle with a little dark Jamaica rum before dotting with butter and baking.

Fresh Corn and Coconut Pudding-Soufflé

If you wish a little more rumness, add a little dark Jamaica rum to the topping butter.

1 cup Thick Coconut Milk (see Index)	2 tablespoons butter
1 cup milk	4 eggs, separated
¾ cup yellow cornmeal	2 tablespoons dark Jamaica rum
1 teaspoon salt	¾ cup cooked fresh corn kernels
¼ teaspoon ground nutmeg (optional)	(or 1 7-ounce can corn, drained)
	Warm melted butter

In a saucepan, heat coconut milk and milk until hot, not boiling. Gradually add cornmeal, stirring constantly. Cook, stirring, until thickened. Remove from heat, add salt, nutmeg, and the 2 tablespoons butter, and stir until blended; set aside to cool slightly. Meantime, beat egg whites until stiff but not dry. Beat yolks, one at a time, into partially cooled cornmeal mixture. Beat in rum. Fold in beaten egg whites along with corn. Turn into a buttered baking dish (about 1½ quarts). Bake in a moderate oven (350°) for 40 minutes or until golden brown. Serve immediately and pass melted butter to ladle over. Makes 4 to 6 servings.

Cranberry Rum Bread

Thick-slice, butter, and broil-toast for a winter breakfast.

2 cups sifted all-purpose flour	1 egg
¾ cup sugar	⅔ cup orange juice
1½ teaspoons baking powder	3 tablespoons dark rum
1 teaspoon salt	2 cups fresh whole cranberries, rinsed and dried
½ teaspoon baking soda	½ cup chopped walnuts or pecans
¼ cup butter	
1 tablespoon grated fresh orange peel	

Sift together into a large mixing bowl the flour, sugar, baking powder, salt, and soda. Cut in butter until mixture resembles coarse cornmeal. Stir in orange peel. Beat egg, then beat in orange juice and rum; add to ingredients in mixing bowl; stir just to blend. Fold in cranberries and nuts. Turn into two small loaf pans (each about 7¼ by 3¼ inches) which have been buttered, lined with waxed paper, and the paper buttered. Bake in a moderate oven (350°) for 1 hour or until rich golden brown and toothpick inserted in center comes out clean. Let bread cool in pan for 5 minutes. Then turn out onto wire racks, remove paper, and allow to cool completely. Wrap in clear plastic wrap or foil and let stand overnight before slicing. Makes 2 small loaves.

FRUIT DESSERTS

Sugared Rum Apple Cake

Serve for a kaffeeklatsch or a rich dessert.

1½ cups sifted all-purpose flour	1 tablespoon dried currants
1 teaspoon sugar	Sugar Topping (recipe below)
1 teaspoon baking powder	Unsweetened whipped cream
½ teaspoon salt	flavored with dark Jamaica
½ cup butter	rum (optional)
1 egg yolk	
2 tablespoons dark rum	
3 large tart cooking apples, peeled, cored, and cut into eighths	

Sift flour, sugar, baking powder, and salt together into mixing bowl. Cut in butter until particles are fine. Beat egg yolk and rum together with a fork, add to ingredients in bowl, and toss with a fork to blend to a dough. With lightly floured fingertips, press dough over bottom and about 1 inch up sides of a 9-inch round layer cake pan. Fill with apples. Sprinkle with currants, then Sugar Topping. Bake in a moderate oven (350°) for about 50 minutes. Cool on a rack to warm. Serve with whipped cream if you wish. Makes 6 to 8 servings.

SUGAR TOPPING

Stir together ¾ cup sugar, 1½ tablespoons flour, ½ teaspoon ground cinnamon, and 2 tablespoons melted butter. Sprinkle over Sugared Rum Apple Cake (above).

Rum Strawberries

Sugar sliced fresh strawberries lightly to sweeten. Sprinkle with enough medium rum to moisten well. Add a few drops of fresh lime juice. Gently toss.

Pineapple Haitienne

Cut extremely thin lengthwise spear slices of fresh pineapple. Arrange, slightly overlapping, in dessert plates. Sprinkle each serving with sugar to sweeten and with 1 to 2 tablespoons Barbancourt rum; let stand for 2 hours. At serving time, pass a soft custard sauce (follow recipe for Soft Custard Rum Sauce [see Index] *except* omit rum and increase vanilla to 1½ teaspoons) to ladle over.

Rum Persimmons

Remove stem from a ripe unpeeled persimmon. Cut in half lengthwise and arrange, cut side up, in a shallow dessert plate. Sprinkle generously with medium rum or dark Jamaica rum, light brown sugar, and a spoonful of sour cream. Spoon out of the shell to eat. Makes 1 serving.

*

Nearly everyone nearly everywhere in the Caribbean has his own idea about how best to do rum bananas. Here are some of those convictions. (See also Madeline's Bananas Flambé [see Index].)

Cool Confection Bananas

2 ripe bananas, peeled and cut
   in half lengthwise
¼ cup honey
¼ cup chopped walnuts
¼ cup commercial sour cream

2 teaspoons sugar
2 teaspoons dark rum
1 teaspoon fresh lime juice
Freshly grated nutmeg (optional)

Arrange banana slices, cut side up, on a platter or two dessert plates. Spoon honey evenly over surfaces. Sprinkle with half of the walnuts. Stir together sour cream, sugar, rum, and lime juice until smooth. Spoon evenly over bananas. Sprinkle with remaining walnuts. Dust lightly with nutmeg if you wish. Chill for 4 hours before serving. Makes 2 servings.

Mrs. Buddles's Baked Bananas Jamaica

Split peeled bananas lengthwise and arrange, cut side up, in a shallow buttered baking dish. Sprinkle lightly with fresh lime juice and generously with sugar. Generously spoon on dark Jamaica rum. Spoon on enough Thick Coconut Milk (see Index) to cloak well. Dot with butter. Bake in a moderate oven (375°) for about 10 minutes. Sprinkle very lightly with lightly toasted finely grated coconut. Serve with the baking syrup spooned over.

Barbecue Rum Bananas

When Sarvis went to the Martinique Hilton, she met the manager, who is a nice guy named Jean-Yves Le Goff. He likes Trader Vic, he likes rum, he is a great fan of Martinique rums, and he has some stout opinions about how to cook with rum. Here is how he said to do bananas.

After you have barbecued some meat, bury whole bananas in skins in the coals. Forget them until they're tender. Then dip bananas into water to wash off ashes. Peel back one strip on each banana. Sprinkle exposed banana with sugar. In a pan on the side, caramelize some sugar. Stand back, add lots of dark rum, flame, and pour over bananas—so all of the sugar caramelizes and flames.

He says this is the *only* way to have banana beignets: Hot, hot beignets (2-inch diagonal pieces) topped with a very cold *sauce anglaise,* and with both the banana batter and the *sauce anglaise* flavored only with fresh vanilla bean. . . . I might also add just a little medium rum to flavor that sauce.

GUYANA AND DESSERTS

I am sitting here chewing the fat with Sarvis about this rum book. She asked me what ever happened to the bottle of El Dorado Blended Reserve rum that she brought back from Guyana for me. And my secretary says, "Trader, don't you remember? You drank it. We had fancy daiquiris all that week, and then you drank the last two golden drops straight." Jeezus, do I remember. It was fabulous! Now, that particular rum doesn't come into this country yet, but I understand that it is going to be imported soon. But even now, look for any Demerara rum by Guyana Distillers Limited, and it will be good.

A nice guy named David Blackman is the mind behind all that rum at Guyana Distillers. And Sarvis tells me that he has a pretty Canadian wife, Madeline, who knows just how to cook with that rum. One day in Georgetown the Blackmans took Sarvis to lunch, along with the distillery's head technologist, David Wells, and his lovely Chinese wife. They talked rum and rum recipes all the time, and to hear Sarvis tell it, it was just as charming as hell. Here are some recipes to prove it.

Madeline's Freezer Cake

Because of the plenteous rum, this dessert is tender and moist and lush when you serve it—not frozen hard.

1 cup soft butter	½ teaspoon vanilla
3 cups sifted powdered sugar	About 12 ounces ladyfingers or
3 eggs	vanilla wafers or Marie
1 tablespoon very strong cool	biscuits
coffee	Lemon Hart Demerara rum

Cream butter and sugar together thoroughly. Add eggs, 1 at a time, and beat until mixture is light and fluffy. Beat in coffee and vanilla. Line a buttered 9-inch spring-form pan or a soufflé dish or charlotte mold (about 2½ quarts) with waxed paper. Dip ¼ of the cookies into rum just to moisten and arrange in a single layer over bottom of pan. Top with ⅓ of the creamed mixture. Repeat twice. Dip remaining cookies in rum and arrange over top. Cover with a plate and put a weight on top. Freeze overnight. Turn out and decorate if you wish and as you wish—possibly with whipped cream and pecans or grated semisweet chocolate. Cut into slender wedges. Makes 12 to 16 servings.

Angela Pia (Pious Angel) from Madeline Blackman

1 envelope (1 tablespoon)
  unflavored gelatin
¼ cup cold water
3 eggs, separated
½ cup sugar

2 tablespoons dark Jamaica rum
2 tablespoons brandy
1 teaspoon vanilla
1 cup heavy (whipping) cream

Sprinkle gelatin into cold water in top part of double boiler and let soften for 5 minutes; then place over hot water and stir until gelatin dissolves completely. Beat egg yolks until light colored. Gradually beat in sugar and beat until thick and light. Beat in rum, brandy, and vanilla. Separately, beat egg whites until stiff but not dry. Whip cream. Beat gelatin thoroughly into egg yolk mixture. Gently but thoroughly fold in beaten whites and cream. Spoon into stemmed dessert glasses. Chill for at least 2 hours. Makes 6 to 8 servings.

Flaming Chocolate Sundaes from Madeline Blackman

1 package (6 ounces) semisweet chocolate chips	**¼ cup light corn syrup**
1 tablespoon butter	**¼ cup dark rum**
¼ cup milk	**1½ pints hard-frozen vanilla, chocolate, or coffee ice cream**

Melt chocolate and butter in top of double boiler over hot, not boiling, water. Gradually stir in milk and syrup and beat until smooth. Pour into a flameproof serving bowl. Heat rum just to warm over very low heat in a small saucepan. Ignite and pour, flaming, into chocolate sauce. Take to table while flaming. When flames subside, stir mixture well. Ladle over ice cream scooped into heatproof sundae glasses or bowls. Makes 1¼ cups sauce, or 4 to 6 servings with ice cream.

Madeline's Bananas Flambé

6 bananas, peeled and halved lengthwise	**¼ cup butter**
2 tablespoons fresh lemon juice	**1 tablespoon grated fresh lemon peel**
½ cup firmly packed light brown sugar	**⅛ teaspoon ground cloves**
¼ teaspoon ground cinnamon	**½ cup Lemon Hart Demerara rum**
¼ teaspoon ground nutmeg	

Arrange bananas, cut side down, in a single layer in a shallow buttered baking dish. Sprinkle with lemon juice. Stir together sugar, cinnamon, and nutmeg and sprinkle over bananas. Dot with butter. Place under broiler until bananas are golden, about 5 minutes. Add lemon peel and cloves to rum and heat it just to warm. Flame and pour over bananas. Makes 6 servings.

*

David Wells knows about all there is to know about the tasting and making of Demerara rums. His wife knows a lot about cooking with it.

Georgetown Spareribs

Purchase Chinese five fragrant spices in powdered form in Chinese markets or specialty food stores.

6 tablespoons dark rum	¼ teaspoon salt
2 tablespoons soy sauce	¼ teaspoon freshly ground black
2 tablespoons honey	pepper
2 tablespoons minced green	2 cloves garlic, minced or mashed
onions (white part only)	1 side pork spareribs (about 3
1½ tablespoons grated fresh	pounds), split in half
ginger	lengthwise and cracked to
½ teaspoon Chinese five fragrant	separate end ribs
spices	

Mix all ingredients together except spareribs. Rub mixture over surfaces of ribs, cover, and chill for 24 hours. Turn occasionally. Place ribs on a rack in a shallow baking pan. Bake in a moderate oven (350°) for 1 hour or until tender and browned, turning occasionally for even browning. Cut into serving-size pieces. Makes 3 to 4 servings.

Demerara Hard Sauce

Demerara sugar is the large-crystal golden sugar made from cane grown in Demerara territory (also the leading territory in Guyana for rum production). It looks much like our raw sugar.

Mr. and Mrs. David Wells, of Georgetown, Guyana, make a crunchy rum hard sauce out of it to drop onto and melt into hot steamed puddings such as dark chocolate, Christmas plum, or pumpkin.

And they intentionally make more of the sauce than they will need for dessert in order to have extra left over to spread onto fresh white bread for tea sandwiches. It is a surprise, and it is good. The sugar gives a crackly new texture, and the total effect is not too sweet. The Wellses like the "touch of the spirit" that the rum gives.

When the Wellses make their hard sauce, they beat butter and Demerara sugar together and gradually add overproof rum until it tastes. They choose overproof rum because it takes less liquid to get the taste. And less liquid helps to keep the grittiness of the sauce— the quality that sets it apart.

If possible, make the following recipe with Demerara sugar (or raw sugar) and overproof rum. If not, use light brown sugar and dark Demerara or Jamaica rum.

Beat ⅓ cup soft butter with 1 cup packed Demerara sugar until well blended. Add 1 egg yolk and beat well. Gradually beat in enough dark rum to flavor the mixture and give a light texture, about 4 teaspoons. Makes about 1 cup.

TWO SPECIAL CAKES

Casablanca Cake

A thousand years ago when I was in Montego Bay, I stayed at the old Casablanca Hotel, where everything was painted white and just spic and span and nice. I don't remember a thing about our dinner that night, but the dessert was out of this stinkin' world.

This Jamaican woman cook had made a *rhum baba*-type raised cake dough and baked it. Then she made a sweet rum sauce with Jamaica rum and apricots and pineapples. Then she poured the sauce over the cake and it went down into it, and, damn it all, it was the best thing I've ever eaten.

She had made her sauce by cooking up dried apricots and fresh pineapple. But today we can get preserves that are just as good.

I would serve this with a glob of whipped cream on top.

Sweet Yeast Cake (recipe below)
Rum Syrup (recipe below)
Pineapple-Apricot Glaze (recipe
  below)

Whipped cream sweetened with
  sugar and flavored with
  vanilla

With a fine skewer, poke holes about every ½ inch over top and down through Sweet Yeast Cake. Slowly pour warm Rum Syrup over warm cake, letting the syrup soak into cake. Cool cake in pan on a rack. Then turn out onto a platter. Slowly spoon enough warm Pineapple-Apricot Glaze over top and sides of cake to glaze. Let cool (and set). Spoon on remaining glaze and let cool. Slice and serve with whipped cream. Makes 12 servings.

SWEET YEAST CAKE

Sprinkle 1 package active dry yeast into ¼ cup warm water, allow to soften, and stir to dissolve. Scald ½ cup milk; add 1 cup butter and stir until butter melts. Stir in ⅓ cup sugar and ¾ teaspoon salt. Allow to cool to lukewarm. In a large bowl, beat 6 eggs until light colored. Stir in yeast mixture and milk mixture. Gradually beat in 3 cups sifted all-purpose flour and beat until batter is smooth. Pour into a well-buttered and lightly floured 3-quart ring mold or a 9-inch bundt pan. Cover with a towel. Let rise in a warm place until almost doubled in bulk, about 1 to 2 hours. Bake in a moderate oven (350°) for 25 to 30 minutes or until toothpick inserted in center comes out clean. Place on a wire rack and let cool for 5 minutes. Use for Casablanca Cake (above).

RUM SYRUP

Combine 2½ cups sugar and 1 cup water in a small saucepan. Heat to boiling, then simmer over medium heat for 6 minutes. Remove from heat and stir in ½ cup dark Jamaica rum and 1 teaspoon vanilla. Use for Casablanca Cake (above).

PINEAPPLE-APRICOT GLAZE

Slowly heat 1 cup apricot-pineapple (or apricot) jam to melt. Remove from heat and stir in ¼ cup dark Jamaica rum. Use for Casablanca Cake (above).

Trinidad Black Rum Cake

Faith Powers is the welcome at the Queen's Park Hotel in Port of Spain. Pretty and British-accented, she is warm receptionist, public relations manager, social director, and procurer of amenities for guests and would-be guests.

Her most joyful experience with rum in Trinidad cookery is black cake. Her mother bakes it. This is the cake that is baked in nearly every established Trinidadian household for any event of significant celebration—always Christmas and also especially for weddings. It is similar to a dark fruitcake, but fully soaked with rum.

Miss Powers's mother bakes the cake. And she keeps the fruit soaking for it from year to year. In telling of it, Miss Powers enthused, "It's almost like a pudding, wet with rum. But it's nothing like a usual rum cake." Then she got so excited that she went to the phone, called her mother for the recipe, and within twenty-four hours, Mommy had baked a cake for Trader Vic to sample.

Here is that cake recipe, just as Mommy wrote it out. The cake itself is velvety and fine, and it is full, full of lush fruit.

The caramel coloring is darkly caramelized sugar dissolved in a little water to make a syrup. The fruits may soak for as long as 1 year.

½ lb. butter	2 tsp. powdered ginger
½ lb. granulated sugar	2 tsp. Angostura
¼ lb. flour	2 tsp. almond essence
6 eggs	2 tsp. vanilla
3 tsp. B. powder	Enough caramel colouring for a
2 tsp. cinnamon	rich brown colour

Beat butter and sugar till creamy, add one egg at a time, then half the flour which has been sifted with other dry ingredients. Now add some of the (drained) fruit which has been soaked for a week or more. When all the flour has been added, pour (in) balance of fruit and as much liquid as it will hold (require) (to make) a wooden spoon just stand in it. Now add essence and colouring and a few glacéed cherries and some slivered almonds. Pour into greased pans lined with greased wax paper and bake in a slow oven for about an hour. Enough for two 9-inch (diameter) by 3-inch-deep pans.

FRUIT TO SOAK:

½ lb. (each) raisins, currants, citron and orange peel, and seeded and chopped prunes. Put in a covered jar with a bottle of rum, one of cherry brandy, and one of port wine. Soak for at least 1 week. Use in Trinidad Black Rum Cake (above).

MRS. LEE'S RECIPES

When I was thinking of where to get my recipes for this book, I naturally thought of the Caribbean. But then one day, I was talking with a good friend of ours, Mrs. Allen Lee, of Hillsborough, California. And I found out that I didn't have to go nearly so far as the West Indies for all rum recipes; I could go right next door. Because when I told Mrs. Lee that I was writing this book, she gave me some of the damnedest recipes. Where she got them I don't know. But they are absolutely fabulous.

Rum Avocado Half Shells

Purely complimentary, quietly.

Cut unpeeled ripe avocados in half and remove pits. Serve each half as a salad with a dressing made in these proportions spooned into cavity: Shake or beat together 3 tablespoons salad oil, 1 tablespoon fresh lime or lemon juice, 1 tablespoon light Puerto Rican rum, about 1 teaspoon snipped fresh chives, and salt and pepper to taste.

Rum Jelly

Stem strawberries make a pretty garnish.

¾ cup water
Peel cut from ¼ lemon and ¼
  orange
1 package (3 ounces)
  lemon-flavored gelatin
1 cup dry white table wine, which
  has been heated through (do
  not boil)

½ cup dark Jamaica rum
Whipped cream lightly sweetened
  with sugar and flavored with
  vanilla

Combine water and lemon and orange peels in a saucepan. Boil uncovered for 5 minutes. Strain over gelatin. Add wine and stir until gelatin is completely dissolved. Stir in rum. Pour into a 1-pint mold (or 4 small dessert cups or pots). Chill until set. At serving time, unmold, cut to serve, and pass cream. Or top with cream. Makes 4 servings.

Plum and Peach Rum Compote

To make when plums and peaches are nice and in season. If you really want to embellish, pass a bowlful of soft custard sauce to ladle on.

Blanch 12 small plums (such as sugar, Santa Rosa, Italian, German, standard) and peel. Blanch 4 large peaches, peel, cut in half, and remove pits. Make a syrup: Combine in a saucepan 3 cups water, 1½ cups sugar, and ½ vanilla bean, split and seeds scraped loose. Heat to boiling, then simmer for about 20 minutes. Remove from heat. Stir in 1 tablespoon fresh lemon juice and 3 tablespoons medium rum. Pour over fruits and chill for 1 day or more. (Be sure to have enough syrup to cover fruit. Gently weigh fruit down under syrup with a plate if necessary to prevent fruit from floating.) Makes 6 generous servings.

Rum-filled Fresh Peaches

It is ultra gilding of the lily, but grand: Add a scoop of rich vanilla ice cream alongside each peach.

6 large freestone peaches
Fresh lemon juice
½ cup macaroon crumbs
2 tablespoons pine nuts
About 2 teaspoons dark Jamaica
  rum

6 fresh mint sprigs
Raspberry Rum Sauce (recipe
  below)

Blanch and peel peaches. Dip into lemon juice to coat well and prevent darkening. Working with a grapefruit knife and keeping peaches whole, gently loosen and remove peach pits. Stir together crumbs, nuts, and enough rum to moisten. Spoon mixture into peach cavities. Cover with transparent plastic wrap and chill for 2 hours or more. At serving time, place each peach, open end down, in a dessert plate. Top with a mint sprig (to resemble a leafed peach). Pass Raspberry Rum Sauce. Makes 6 servings.

RASPBERRY RUM SAUCE

Combine in a saucepan 1 package (10 ounces) frozen red raspberries, ½ cup red currant jelly, ¼ cup sugar, 1 tablespoon cornstarch, and a pinch of salt. Bring to a boil, reduce heat, and simmer for about 5 minutes. Strain and stir in 1 tablespoon dark Jamaica rum and 1 teaspoon fresh lemon juice. Serve with Rum-filled Fresh Peaches (above). Makes about 1¼ cups.

Mrs. Lee's Chocolate Rum Sauce

Serve warm over vanilla or lemon or coffee ice cream, or a chocolate sponge roll, or whatever.

Not to betray rum, but: Sometimes Mrs. Lee flavors it with 4 tablespoons sweet sherry and 1 teaspoon brandy instead of the rum and vanilla.

If you make this ahead: Reheat over simmering water in top part of double boiler.

1½ cups sugar

3 tablespoons butter

4 ounces (4 squares) unsweetened
baking chocolate

1 cup heavy (whipping) cream

4 tablespoons dark Jamaica rum

1 teaspoon vanilla

Combine sugar, butter, chocolate, and cream in a heavy saucepan. Cook and stir until mixture blends and comes to a boil. Then gently boil without stirring for 7 minutes. Remove from heat and stir in rum and vanilla. Makes at least 2 cups sauce.

Fudgey Pots de Crème

If necessary to make these ahead, chill, then return to room temperature before serving.

1 package (8 ounces) semisweet
chocolate

¼ cup strong coffee

4 eggs, separated

2 teaspoons dark Jamaica rum

Heat chocolate and coffee together in top part of double boiler placed over simmering water just until chocolate melts. Stir until smooth. Turn into a mixing bowl. Beat egg yolks slightly and stir into chocolate mixture. Beat egg whites until stiff but not dry and fold in. Fold in rum. Spoon into 6 *pot de crème* pots or small dessert cups. Serve at room temperature. Makes 6 servings.

Cold Pumpkin Soufflé

1 envelope (1 tablespoon)
unflavored gelatin

¼ cup dark Jamaica rum

4 eggs

½ teaspoon vanilla

⅔ cup sugar

1 cup canned or cooked and
puréed pumpkin

½ teaspoon ground cinnamon

½ teaspoon ground ginger

¼ teaspoon ground mace

¼ teaspoon ground cloves

1/16 teaspoon salt

1 cup heavy cream, whipped stiff

Candied fruits, slivered candied
ginger, or a dusting of nutmeg

Whipped cream lightly sweetened
with sugar and flavored with
vanilla

Sprinkle gelatin over rum in top part of double boiler. Allow to soften. Place over hot water and stir until gelatin is completely dissolved; set aside. Beat eggs until thick and lemon-colored. Beat in vanilla. Gradually add sugar and beat until mixture is smooth and very thick. Stir together pumpkin, cinnamon, ginger, mace, cloves, and salt; stir into egg mixture. Whisk in gelatin thoroughly. Fold in the 1 cup cream, whipped. Butter a 6-inch band of waxed paper and use it to line a buttered 1-quart soufflé dish (buttered side in) so that about 3 inches of paper extends above rim of dish. Turn in pumpkin mixture. Chill until set. Garnish with candied fruits, candied ginger, or nutmeg at serving time. Serve with the sweetened whipped cream. Makes about 6 servings.

DESSERT OMELETS

Omelet Jamaique, Terra Nova

Make a very moist Basic Omelet (recipe below) *except:* Before folding, spoon 2 tablespoons strawberry preserves down center. Fold and roll out of pan into a warm flameproof platter. Sprinkle lightly with finely chopped pistachios. In a small pan or a ladle, warm 2 to 3 tablespoons dark Jamaica rum. Ignite and pour over omelet. Ladle flaming rum over omelet until flames die. Serve with syrup spooned over. Makes 1 serving.

Brown-sugared Rum Omelet

Stir together 3 tablespoons packed light brown sugar, 1 tablespoon finely chopped pecans, and 2 teaspoons melted butter. Make a very moist Basic Omelet (recipe below). Roll out of pan into flameproof platter. Sprinkle with sugar mixture. In a small pan or a ladle, warm 3 tablespoons dark Jamaica rum. Ignite and pour over omelet. Ladle flaming rum high and over omelet until flames die. Serve with syrup spooned over. Makes 1 serving.

Basic Omelet

Beat 2 eggs, 2 teaspoons water, and ⅛ teaspoon salt vigorously with a fork until blended. Melt 2 teaspoons butter in an 8-inch omelet pan over medium-high heat until it bubbles and begins to brown. Pour eggs into pan and tilt pan so egg covers bottom. Lift egg edges with a thin-bladed spatula and tilt pan so uncooked egg flows to bottom of pan; cook until top is still creamy but barely set. Fold top third of omelet over filling and slip omelet out of pan onto warm serving plate, rolling pan so that folded section falls over its extended edge. Makes 1 serving.

Cake Crouton Omelet

Make croutons: Cut day-old sponge cake or pound cake into ½-inch cubes; measure ¾ cup. In a frying pan over low heat, gently sauté cubes in about 1½ tablespoons butter until crisp and golden brown.

Make apricot-rum sauce: Slowly melt 3 tablespoons apricot jam. Stir in ⅛ teaspoon grated fresh orange peel and ¾ teaspoon dark Jamaica rum and barely heat through. Make Basic Omelet (recipe above) *except:* Before folding, spoon croutons down center. Fold and slip onto serving plate. Spoon on a little of the apricot sauce and add more as you wish. Makes 1 generous serving.

THE VANILLA RUM IDEA

Vanilla Rum

You know, vanilla is really the basis for tying all flavors together in cakes and baked sweets. And vanilla extract is difficult to come by in Haiti. So a Haitian hostess told Shirley her secret in making rum desserts. She (and many another smart cook) puts a fresh vanilla bean into a bottle of rum—to extend the vanilla and to make her own vanilla flavoring. You can make it, too; and use your vanilla rum instead of usual vanilla extract or flavoring in your baking.

Also, vanilla rum can be part of a special dessert coffee.

Split a vanilla bean, put it into a good-looking decanter, and fill decanter with your favorite rum (or just put split vanilla bean into bottle of rum). Cover and let stand for at least 2 days—or indefinitely.

Rum Cream Coffee

Pour freshly brewed hot black coffee into each cup. Pass vanilla rum and a bowlful of lightly sweetened whipped cream. Let each guest add rum and cream to coffee as he wishes.

COOL DESSERTS

Spanish Cream (Lime, Lemon, or Orange)

The idea for the Lime Spanish Cream with warm chocolate rum sauce came from Mrs. David Wells, of Guyana. The idea for the three possible citrus flavors and their possible sauces came from Hamish Gordon, of the Ocean View Hotel in Barbados.

With lime cream: Serve a warm chocolate rum sauce (your own chocolate sauce or commercial sauce with a little dark rum added, or Mrs. Lee's Chocolate Rum Sauce [see Index]), or whipped cream lightly sweetened with sugar and flavored with dark rum and vanilla, or a warm strawberry sauce which has been lightly spiced with ground allspice and dark rum, or warm raspberry rum sauce (your own recipe or Raspberry Rum Sauce [see Index] with a little ground nutmeg added).

With lemon cream: Serve a warm tart black currant sauce lightly spiced with dark Jamaica rum.

With orange cream: Serve whipped cream lightly sweetened and flavored with dark Jamaica rum and vanilla.

1 envelope (1 tablespoon) unflavored gelatin
½ cup sugar
¼ teaspoon salt
3 eggs, separated
3 cups milk
1 tablespoon grated fresh lime peel or 1½ tablespoons fresh lemon peel or 2 tablespoons fresh orange peel

1 teaspoon fresh lime, lemon, or orange juice
1 teaspoon vanilla
1 teaspoon dark Jamaica rum

In top of double boiler, mix gelatin, ¼ cup of the sugar, and the salt. Stir in egg yolks, then gradually stir in milk. Cook over boiling water, stirring constantly, until mixture is smooth and very slightly thickened and coats a silver spoon. Chill until slightly thicker than unbeaten egg white; stir in citrus peel, juice, vanilla, and rum. Beat egg whites until foamy. Beat in remaining ¼ cup sugar, adding it about 1 tablespoon at a time; beat until whites are stiff and glossy. Fold in gelatin mixture. Leave in bowl or turn into 8 individual molds or custard cups. Chill until set. At serving time, spoon into dessert glasses or unmold. Makes 8 servings.

Golden Rum Zabaglione

6 egg yolks
6 tablespoons sugar
½ teaspoon grated fresh lemon
  peel

6 tablespoons medium rum

Beat egg yolks, sugar, and lemon peel together in top of double boiler. Place over hot (not boiling) water and gradually beat in rum. Cook, beating constantly with a wire whisk, until thick, light, and smooth, about 5 to 10 minutes. Pour into small stemmed glasses and serve immediately, or chill. Makes 4 servings.

Pots of Key Lime Custard

3 egg yolks
1 can (15 ounces) sweetened
  condensed milk
½ cup fresh lime juice
1 tablespoon dark Jamaica rum

1 teaspoon grated fresh lime peel
Softly whipped cream lightly
  sweetened with sugar and
  flavored with vanilla

Beat egg yolks and milk together until smooth. Add lime juice and rum and beat until mixture is smooth and thickened. Stir in lime peel. Turn into 6 small dessert dishes, pots, or glasses. Chill if you wish. At serving time, top each serving with a spoonful of whipped cream. Makes 6 servings.

Laced Lime Cream Sherbet

Use a light hand with the rum. Any more than a little covers rather than enhances the lime.

2 eggs	2 teaspoons grated fresh lime
½ cup sugar	peel
½ cup light corn syrup	¼ cup fresh lime juice
2 cups half and half (half milk	Medium rum
and half cream)	Thin lime slices

Beat eggs and sugar together until thick and light colored. Stir in syrup, half and half, lime peel, and juice. Freeze until almost firm. Beat until smooth, return to freezer, and freeze firm (or beat once more before freezing firm). At serving time, scoop into chilled dessert glasses and spoon on just a little rum. Garnish each serving with a lime slice. Makes about 1 quart sherbet, or 6 servings.

Bitters Glowing Sundae

This idea came from a Trinidadian fan of good food who now lives in Barbados. His loyalty to Trinidad bitters shows.

Scoop rum raisin ice cream into chilled stemmed dessert glasses. Top each serving with a generous drizzling of Angostura bitters.

Kona Ice Cream

For each serving: Put 1 large scoop of rich vanilla or coconut ice cream into a large sherbet glass. Halve 2 fresh or canned ring slices of pineapple and arrange around base of ice cream. Cut half of a banana in half, lengthwise, and place pieces against two sides of the ice cream. Sprinkle with shredded coconut. Place in a small pan 1 tablespoon pineapple-apricot jam, 1½ tablespoons light Puerto Rican rum, and 1½ teaspoons dark Jamaica rum. Heat to warm, ignite, and spoon the flaming liquid high over jam until flames die. Stir jam and remaining liquid in pan together, ladle over ice cream, and serve immediately.

Tahitian Ice Cream

For each serving: Place a warm individual *rhum baba* in a dessert plate. Top with a scoop of coconut ice cream. Ladle the following sauce over ice cream and serve the dessert immediately: Place in a small pan 1 tablespoon pineapple-apricot jam, 1½ tablespoons light Puerto Rican rum, and 1½ teaspoons dark Jamaica rum. Heat to warm, ignite, and spoon the flaming liquid high over jam until flames die. Stir jam and remaining liquid in pan together.

Deep Rum Vanilla

1 pint hand-packed rich vanilla ice cream
½ cup light Puerto Rican rum

Press ice cream into 8 small ramekins or *pot de crème* pots. Freeze firm. Before serving, pour 1 tablespoon rum on top of each. Makes 8 servings.

Coconut Ice Cream

Serve with a topping of Hot Butter-rum Cream (recipe below) or fresh red currants which have been lightly crushed with sugar to sweeten and dark Jamaica rum to flavor.

3-inch piece vanilla bean	**¼ teaspoon salt**
1½ cups milk	**2 cups grated fresh coconut**
4 slightly beaten egg yolks	**1½ cups heavy (whipping) cream**
¾ cup sugar	

Scrape seeds from vanilla bean into milk in a saucepan. Add vanilla pod. Scald milk. Mix together in top of double boiler the egg yolks, sugar, and salt. Beat in hot milk, a little at a time. Cook over hot water, stirring, until mixture is thickened and smooth. Remove vanilla pod. Stir in coconut. Chill. Stir in cream. Freeze in a hand-crank or electric freezer (or turn into a freezer tray to freeze; stir twice before freezing firm). Makes about 1½ quarts.

Hot Butter-rum Cream

Combine in a saucepan ½ cup sugar, ½ cup heavy cream, and ¼ cup butter. Heat to a full rolling boil. Remove from heat and stir in 2 tablespoons light Puerto Rican rum and a pinch of ground cardamom. Serve with Coconut Ice Cream (above). Makes about 1⅓ cups.

Calabash Coconut Ice Cream

From Calabash Restaurant, Montego Bay.

3-inch piece vanilla bean
1 cup Thick Coconut Milk (see Index)
½ cup regular milk
4 slightly beaten egg yolks
¾ cup sugar
¼ teaspoon salt
1½ cups heavy (whipping) cream
2 tablespoons light rum
Fine julienne strips of fresh coconut

Scrape seeds from vanilla bean into coconut milk and regular milk in a saucepan. Add vanilla pod. Scald milk. Mix together in top of double boiler the egg yolks, sugar, and salt. Beat in hot milk, a little at a time. Cook over hot water, stirring, until mixture is thickened and smooth. Chill. Remove vanilla pod. Stir in cream and rum. Freeze in a hand-crank or electric freezer (or turn into a freezer tray to freeze; stir twice before freezing firm). To serve, scoop into chilled dessert glasses and top with a light sprinkling of coconut. Makes about 1 quart.

Rum Butterscotch Ice Cream Cakes

Bake good yellow butter cake or sponge cake cupcakes. Split each in half, crosswise, and fill with a thick layer of rich vanilla ice cream. When ice cream begins to soften, turn each cake upside down in a dessert plate (so it will resemble a pastry, not a cupcake). Top generously with warm Rum Butterscotch Sauce (recipe below).

Rum Butterscotch Sauce

In a small saucepan, melt ¼ cup butter. Stir in ¾ cup firmly packed light brown sugar and 1 tablespoon light corn syrup. Heat to a gentle boil and cook, stirring, until sugar melts. Gradually stir in ¼ cup heavy (whipping) cream, and return to a boil. Remove from heat and stir in 1 tablespoon dark Jamaica rum. Serve with Rum Butterscotch Ice Cream Cakes (above). Makes about 1 cup.

Rum Brownie Dessert

This is a rich and sensational dessert based on all-American brownies. While brownies are still a little warm from baking, cut them into big squares or wedges, score across the top, pour on enough medium rum to soak in well, and top or side with scoops of rich vanilla ice cream. The rum seems to intensify and add a richer bitterness to the chocolate taste. Be fairly generous with the rum addition.

Here is the basic brownie recipe that we start with. It provides the base for 8 to 10 dessert servings.

2 squares (2 ounces) unsweetened chocolate	1 teaspoon vanilla
½ cup butter	1/16 teaspoon salt
2 eggs	½ cup unsifted all-purpose flour
1 cup sugar	½ cup chopped walnuts

Melt chocolate and butter in top of a double boiler placed over simmering water. Set aside and let cool. Beat eggs until thick and lemon-colored. Beat in sugar, 1 tablespoon at a time, and beat until very thick. Beat in vanilla and salt. Beat in melted chocolate and butter. Add flour and beat at low speed just until blended. Stir in nuts. Turn into a buttered 8-inch square baking pan or a 9-inch round layer cake pan with removable bottom. Bake in a slow oven (325°) for 32 minutes, until toothpick inserted in center comes out clean. (Do not overbake.) Cool on a rack. Cut into bars or wedges.

Spiced Apple Tortoni

2 tart cooking apples, peeled and shredded or finely chopped	¼ teaspoon ground cinnamon
⅓ cup sugar	¼ teaspoon ground mace
2 eggs	½ teaspoon fresh lemon juice
1/16 teaspoon salt	1 cup heavy (whipping) cream
½ cup sugar	2 tablespoons dark Jamaica rum
¼ cup water	Zwieback crumbs

Place apples in a heavy pan with the ⅓ cup sugar and cook uncovered over low heat until apples are tender; stir occasionally; cool. Beat eggs with salt until light and fluffy. Combine the ½ cup sugar and the water in a saucepan. Heat to boiling and boil for 3 minutes without stirring. Immediately pour hot syrup in a fine stream into beaten eggs, beating constantly. Turn into top of double boiler and cook over hot water, stirring constantly, until mixture is thick and smooth and increased in volume. Remove from heat, set pan in a bowl of cold water, and continue stirring until cool. Stir in cinnamon, mace, and lemon juice. Stir in apples. Beat cream, gradually adding rum, until whipped; fold in. Spoon into individual fluted paper cups, sprinkle top of each generously with zwieback crumbs, and freeze quickly until firm. Makes 8 to 10 servings.

Rum Raisin Parfait

Like rum raisin ice cream, this is good served topped with a good dash of Angostura bitters.

½ cup dark or golden seedless raisins	1 cup sugar
	½ cup water
6 tablespoons dark Jamaica rum	1 teaspoon fresh lemon juice
4 eggs	½ teaspoon vanilla
⅛ teaspoon salt	2 cups heavy cream, whipped

Soak raisins in rum at room temperature until raisins are plump, about 12 hours. Beat eggs with salt until light and fluffy. Combine sugar and water in a saucepan. Heat to boiling and boil for 3 minutes without stirring. Beating constantly, pour hot syrup in a fine stream into beaten eggs. Pour mixture into top of double boiler and cook over hot water, stirring constantly, until mixture is thick and smooth and increased in volume. Remove from heat, set pan in a bowl of cold water, and continue stirring until cool. Stir in lemon juice, vanilla, and plumped raisins with rum. Fold in whipped cream. Freeze quickly until firm. Cover. Makes about 1½ quarts, or 12 servings.

Rum Frango

Follow directions for Rum Raisin Parfait (above) *except* omit raisins and use only 4 tablespoons dark Jamaica rum.

DESSERT CRÊPES

Crêpes Josephine

The Martinique Hilton designed this for breakfast, but they didn't put rum in it. We like it for breakfast or for dessert with a scoop of vanilla ice cream alongside.

2 Crêpes (recipe below)
2 lengthwise slices of ripe
 banana, each ¼ inch thick

1 tablespoon butter
3 tablespoons honey
1 tablespoon dark Jamaica rum

Roll each crêpe around a banana slice and arrange side by side in a heatproof plate. Dot crepes with butter. Stir honey and rum together and drizzle over crêpes. Broil about 6 inches from heat until bubbly and heated through. Serve crêpes with sauce spooned over. Makes 1 serving.

Crêpes

Beat 3 eggs slightly. Add 6 tablespoons flour and ⅜ teaspoon salt and beat until smooth. Gradually add 1 cup milk, beating until batter is smooth. Cover and chill for 30 minutes if possible; stir to blend well before using. Heat butter (½ to 1 teaspoon for each crêpe) over medium-high heat in a 7- to 8-inch crêpe pan. Pour in about 3 tablespoons batter; quickly tilt and rotate pan so batter covers bottom. When lightly brown on bottom, turn and lightly brown on second side. Slip onto plate or clean towel. Makes about 12 crêpes.

Flaming Banana Crêpes

These dessert crêpes are also fine without the bananas.

⅓ cup butter
½ cup sugar
Grated peel of 1 orange
¼ cup fresh orange juice
2 teaspoons fresh lemon juice
16 slices banana, each about 2
 inches long and 3/16 inch
 thick (cut banana lengthwise or
 on a long diagonal)

8 Crêpes (recipe above)
¼ cup dark Jamaica rum
¼ cup finely chopped lightly
 toasted pecans
¾ cup heavy cream, softly
 whipped with 1 tablespoon
 sugar and ¾ teaspoon vanilla

In a large chafing dish set over medium-low flame (or in a large frying pan over medium-low heat), melt butter. Stir in sugar, orange peel, orange juice, and lemon juice; stir until sugar melts. Inserting

2 banana slices in each, fold each crêpe in half twice (to make quarter-circle shape). Place in chafing dish; spoon syrup over them. Add rum to ladle or at edge of pan and as soon as it warms, light it. Spoon flaming syrup over crêpes, lifting it high to allow air to reach it. When flames die, arrange 2 crêpes, slightly overlapping, on each dessert plate; spoon syrup over, sprinkle with pecans, and put a spoonful of whipped cream alongside. Makes 4 servings.

SAUCES AND TOPPINGS

Soft Custard Rum Sauce

This is a lovely basic soft custard sauce to lavish onto anything that responds well to such—pound cake, sliced fresh fruits, poached dried fruits, warm apple pudding. One of the best ways to use it is ladled generously over sliced bananas and/or sliced fresh strawberries, then sprinkled with Lace Praline (recipe below).

Beat together thoroughly in top of double boiler 4 egg yolks, 2 cups half and half (half milk and half cream), ¼ cup sugar, and ⅛ teaspoon salt. Cook over hot water, stirring, until mixture thickens slightly and coats a silver spoon. Strain custard. Stir in 2 tablespoons medium rum and 1 teaspoon vanilla. Allow to cool, stirring occasionally. Cover and chill. Makes about 2 cups.

Lace Praline

Thickly butter a chilled baking sheet. Sprinkle with ⅛-to-¼-inch-thick layer of brown sugar which has been rubbed through a strainer. Broil about 6 inches beneath heat until sugar bubbles; watch carefully. Cool until slightly hardened. Loosen and ease off sheet with a flexible spatula. Cool. Break into small pieces. Sprinkle over Soft Custard Rum Sauce (above).

Coconut Eggnog Sauce

A plush dessert sauce to drift over a few chilled preserved kumquats (cut open and seeded and replaced in whole shape) or fresh raspberries or rich vanilla or coffee ice cream.

2 egg yolks	**¾ cup toasted grated fresh**
¾ cup unsifted powdered sugar	**coconut**
2 tablespoons dark Jamaica rum	**Ground nutmeg (optional)**
1 cup heavy cream, whipped	

Beat egg yolks with sugar until light and fluffy. Beat in rum. Fold in whipped cream and coconut. Sprinkle with nutmeg. Makes sauce for 6 servings.

To toast coconut: Spread grated fresh coconut over a baking sheet. Bake in a slow over (300°), stirring frequently, until lightly browned, about 20 minutes.

Creamy Rum Sauce

This is a good quick sauce for topping apple beignets or a warm apple-nut loaf cake.

Melt ¼ cup butter in a saucepan. Add ½ cup heavy (whipping) cream, ½ cup sugar, and $\frac{1}{16}$ teaspoon salt. Bring to a full rolling boil, stirring. Remove from heat and stir in 2 tablespoons medium rum.

Quick Ice Cream Sauce

You don't even have to heat this.

Stir crunchy peanut butter until smooth with enough dark corn syrup to sweeten and enough dark Jamaica rum to thin.

Mellow Chocolate Icing

The icing recipe comes from Hamish Gordon, Ocean View Hotel, Barbados. He suggests that you frost it over a fresh lemon or lime or orange cake. Then both the cake and the icing are light enough for one another.

Beat ½ pound soft butter until creamy. Gradually beat in 2½ cups sifted powdered sugar and 4 tablespoons unsifted cocoa powder until mixture is soft and creamy. Gradually add 4 teaspoons dark Jamaica rum and beat until smooth. Makes frosting to cover 1 deep 10-inch sponge cake.

PUDDINGS AND CAKES

Corn puddings abound in the Caribbean. And almost all of them owe much of their tastiness to rum-plumped raisins in them.

The Indian pudding considered Early American appears in the U. S. Virgin Islands as corn pudding; and the rum raisins are part of it.

Raisin Corn Pudding

Make Indian pudding according to your favorite recipe *except* before baking, add dark raisins which have been soaked in dark rum until plump (12 to 24 hours) and drained.

Jamaican Corn Pudding

Jamaican corn puddings often call for Thick Coconut Milk (see Index) instead of regular milk. If you wish, serve this with sweetened whipped cream lightly flavored with vanilla.

1 cup dark seedless raisins	1¼ cups cold water
1 cup dark Jamaica rum	1⅔ cups milk
1 cup yellow cornmeal	¾ cup butter
1½ tablespoons flour	4 eggs
1 teaspoon ground cinnamon	1½ cups sugar
1 teaspoon ground nutmeg	1½ teaspoons vanilla
½ teaspoon salt	Fresh or maraschino cherries

Soak raisins in rum for 12 to 24 hours. Drain, saving rum. Stir together cornmeal, flour, cinnamon, nutmeg, and salt. Stir in water. In a large saucepan, heat milk to boiling. Gradually whisk in cornmeal mixture. Cook, whisking, until mixture comes to a full boil. Then cook over medium heat, stirring, for 5 minutes. Remove from heat. Add butter and stir to melt. Beat eggs until thick and light colored. Gradually add all except 2 tablespoons of the sugar and beat until mixture is smooth and very thick. Beat in vanilla. Gradually beat in cornmeal mixture. Beat in 1 tablespoon of the reserved rum. Stir in raisins. Turn into a buttered 9-inch spring-form pan. Sprinkle with remaining 2 tablespoons sugar. Bake in a moderate oven (350°) for 1½ hours or until set and deep golden brown and knife inserted in center comes out clean. Cool on rack in pan to lukewarm or room temperature. Gently loosen sides of spring-form pan. Cut pudding into wedges. Decorate each serving with a cherry. Makes about 18 servings.

Round Rum Saturates

Serve immediately out of the oven.

1 cup sifted flour
½ cup sugar
½ teaspoon baking powder
½ teaspoon baking soda
½ teaspoon salt
¼ cup soft butter
⅓ cup buttermilk
1 egg

4 teaspoons grated fresh orange
  peel
1 cup moist dates, cut up
Orange syrup of ⅔ cup fresh
  orange juice mixed with ⅓
  cup sugar and 3 tablespoons
  dark Jamaica rum

Sift flour, the ½ cup sugar, the baking powder, soda, and salt together into mixing bowl. Add butter, buttermilk, and egg and beat until smooth. Stir in orange peel and dates. Spoon into 8 or 9 buttered muffin cups. Bake in a moderate oven (350°) for about 25 to 30 minutes or until deep golden. Place a cake upside down in each dessert plate. Slowly spoon syrup over, letting it soak in. Serve immediately. Makes 8 or 9 servings.

Fresh Pineapple Upside-down Cake

⅓ cup butter
½ cup firmly packed light brown
  sugar
2 tablespoons granulated sugar
½ teaspoon grated fresh lemon
  peel
¼-inch-thick ring slices of fresh
  pineapple, cored

Pecan halves or chopped pecans
  (optional)
Cake Batter (recipe below)
Barbancourt 3-star or 5-star rum
  or Lemon Hart Demerara rum
Unsweetened whipped cream

Melt butter in bottom of a heavy 10-inch frying pan or a 9-inch-square baking pan. Stir together brown sugar, granulated sugar, and lemon peel; sprinkle evenly over butter. Arrange pineapple slices close together in a decorative pattern over sugar. Add pecans if you wish. Pour Cake Batter over fruit. Bake in a moderate oven (350°) for 40 to 50 minutes or until toothpick inserted in center comes out clean. Immediately turn upside down onto serving platter; leave pan over cake for a few minutes. Serve while warm. Drizzle a spoonful of rum over each serving and let it soak in. Pass whipped cream. Makes 8 servings.

CAKE BATTER

Sift together into a mixing bowl 1⅓ cups sifted all-purpose flour, 1 cup sugar, 2 teaspoons baking powder, and ½ teaspoon salt. Add ⅓ cup soft butter, ⅔ cup milk, and 1 teaspoon vanilla. Beat until very smooth, about 2 minutes. Add 1 egg and beat for 2 minutes more. Use for Fresh Pineapple Upside-down Cake (above).

Vanilla Rum Cake and Ice Cream with Rum Apricot Sauce

⅓ cup ground walnuts
3 tablespoons sifted light brown sugar
2 cups sifted all-purpose flour
1¾ cups sugar
1 teaspoon baking powder
1 teaspoon baking soda
½ teaspoon salt
1 egg

1 cup buttermilk
⅔ cup melted butter
1 teaspoon vanilla
6 tablespoons medium rum
Rich vanilla ice cream (about 1½ to 2 pints hand-packed)
Rum Apricot Sauce (recipe below)

Stir together nuts and brown sugar. Sprinkle into a thickly buttered 8- or 9-inch bundt pan and shake to coat pan sides. Sift together into a large mixing bowl the flour, sugar, baking powder, soda, and salt. Beat egg, then beat in buttermilk, butter, and vanilla; add to flour mixture and beat with a spoon until smooth. Turn into prepared pan. Bake in a moderate oven (350°) for 55 to 60 minutes or until toothpick inserted in center comes out clean. With a fine skewer, poke holes about every ½ inch over top and down through warm cake; slowly spoon rum over cake, letting it soak into cake. Cool in pan on a rack. When cool, cover tightly and allow to stand for at least 12 hours. With a thin knife, loosen cake at edges and turn out. Wrap in foil and reheat in oven before serving. (Or reheat foil-covered cake in pan, then turn out. Or slice cake and wrap slices in foil to reheat.) Serve warm slices onto individual dessert plates with ice cream alongside. Pass warm apricot sauce to be ladled over cake and, if you wish, over ice cream. Makes about 12 servings.

RUM APRICOT SAUCE

Melt 1 cup apricot jam over low heat in a saucepan. Stir in ½ teaspoon grated fresh orange peel and 3 tablespoons medium rum and barely heat through. Makes about 1 cup. Serve with Vanilla Rum Cake and Ice Cream (above). NOTE: If you like a lot of sauce, make 1½ times the recipe. (Previously published in *Woman's Day*.)

Orange Pecan Crown Cake

Garnish served cake slices with fresh stem strawberries and a small mound of powdered sugar for dipping alongside.

6 tablespoons soft butter	**Grated peel of 1 large orange**
½ cup sugar	**2 tablespoons flour**
1 egg	**6 tablespoons finely cut dates**
½ teaspoon vanilla	**½ cup finely chopped pecans**
1 cup sifted all-purpose flour	**6 tablespoons fresh orange juice**
½ teaspoon baking powder	**¼ cup sugar**
½ teaspoon baking soda	**2 tablespoons medium rum**
⅛ teaspoon salt	**Powdered sugar**
½ cup buttermilk	

In a mixing bowl, cream together butter and the ½ cup sugar thoroughly. Add egg and vanilla and beat until mixture is light and fluffy. Sift together the 1 cup flour, baking powder, soda, and salt; beat into creamed mixture alternately with buttermilk. Stir in orange peel. Stir together the 2 tablespoons flour, dates, and pecans; add to batter and stir until smooth. Turn into a buttered 8-inch (4- to 6-cup) kugelhopf pan (or other tubed cake pan without removable bottom, about 1-quart size). Bake in a moderate oven (350°) for 50 minutes or until cake springs back when lightly touched with fingertip. With a fine skewer, poke holes about every ½ inch over top and down through cake. Stir together orange juice, the ¼ cup sugar, and rum; slowly spoon over warm cake, letting the syrup soak into cake. Cool cake in pan on a rack. When cool, cover or wrap tightly and allow to stand for 2 to 3 days. With a thin knife, loosen cake at edges and turn out. Dust with sifted powdered sugar. Gently cut into fairly thick slices. Makes about 8 servings.

Pam's Karithopeta

¾ cup soft butter
¾ cup sugar
3 eggs
1 cup sifted all-purpose flour
1½ teaspoons baking powder
¾ teaspoon ground cinnamon
⅜ teaspoon ground nutmeg

¼ teaspoon salt
¼ cup milk
1½ teaspoons grated fresh
  orange peel
1 cup finely chopped walnuts
Honey Syrup (recipe below)

In a large mixing bowl, beat butter and sugar together until thoroughly creamed. Add eggs, 1 at a time, beating well after each addition. Sift together flour, baking powder, cinnamon, nutmeg, and salt. Beat into creamed mixture alternately with milk, beginning and ending with dry ingredients. Stir in orange peel and nuts. Spread in a buttered 8-inch-square baking pan. Bake in a moderate oven (350°) for 40 to 45 minutes or until cake springs back when touched lightly with a fingertip. While hot, cut cake into diamond shapes. Slowly pour syrup over. Cool on a rack. Serve immediately or cover and refrigerate until ready to use. (It keeps well.) Makes 20 whole diamond-shaped pieces.

HONEY SYRUP

Stir together ⅔ cup sugar, ⅔ cup mild honey, and ⅓ cup water in a saucepan. Heat to boiling, then simmer for 5 minutes. Skim off white foam. Stir in ¼ teaspoon ground cinnamon, 4 teaspoons dark Jamaica rum, and 2 teaspoons fresh lemon juice. Simmer for 2 minutes more. Cool. Use with Pam's Karithopeta (above). (Previously published in *Chevron USA*.)

Rum Trifle

1 round sponge cake layer, about
  6 ounces and 8 or 9 inches in
  diameter
6 tablespoons Barbancourt 5-star
  (or medium or dark) rum
About ¾ pound crisp almond
  macaroons

2 large cans (1 pound, 14 ounces
  each) peeled whole apricots,
  well drained, halved, and
  pitted
Coffee Custard Sauce (recipe
  below)
1 cup heavy (whipping) cream

2 tablespoons sugar
½ teaspoon vanilla
¼ cup lightly toasted sliced
  almonds

Place cake layer in bottom of a handsome crystal serving bowl, about 2½ to 3 quarts. Sprinkle evenly with 4 tablespoons of the rum. Arrange half of the macaroons over cake and sprinkle with 1 tablespoon of the rum. Arrange half of the apricots over macaroons. Top with remaining macaroons, sprinkle with the remaining tablespoon of rum, and top with remaining apricots. Pour cooled custard sauce evenly over all. Cover and chill for 4 to 24 hours. At serving time, beat cream with sugar and vanilla until softly whipped; swirl over top of trifle. Sprinkle with almonds. Spoon out to serve. Makes 10 servings.

COFFEE CUSTARD SAUCE

Beat together thoroughly in top part of double boiler 4 egg yolks, 2 cups half and half (half milk and half cream), ¼ cup sugar, and ⅛ teaspoon salt. Cook over hot (not boiling) water, stirring, until mixture thickens slightly and coats a silver spoon. Strain. Stir in 1½ teaspoons instant coffee powder (or instant coffee crystals crushed to a powder) and ½ teaspoon vanilla. Allow to cool, stirring occasionally. Use for Rum Trifle (above).

Rummed Bread Pudding

2¼ cups milk	**¼ teaspoon salt**
2 slightly beaten eggs	**1½ tablespoons dark Jamaica**
2 cups of ½-inch dices of day-old	**rum**
farm-style white bread	**1 teaspoon vanilla**
½ cup firmly packed brown sugar	**½ cup seedless raisins**
⅜ teaspoon ground nutmeg	**2 tablespoons melted butter**
⅜ teaspoon ground cinnamon	**Whipped cream**

Combine milk and eggs and pour over bread cubes. Stir in remaining ingredients except cream. Pour into an 8-inch round buttered baking dish (about 1¼ quarts). Set into a pan with hot water about 1 inch deep in bottom. Bake in a moderate oven (350°) until silver knife inserted halfway between center and outside comes out clean, about 45 to 50 minutes. Let cool to lukewarm. Spoon into serving dishes. Top with whipped cream. Makes about 5 servings.

Royalty Rum Pudding

5 eggs	3 tablespoons dark Jamaica rum
1¼ cups sugar	Grated semisweet chocolate

Beat eggs and sugar together until sugar is dissolved. Beat in rum. Pour into a shallow baking dish (3- to 4-cup size, so pudding is about 1 inch deep). Set into a pan with hot water ½ to 1 inch deep in bottom. Bake in a slow oven (325°) for 35 minutes or just until set. Remove from water; cool on a rack. Spoon into dessert dishes and sprinkle lightly with chocolate. Makes 5 servings.

Trader Vic's Macadamia Nut Wisp

4 extra-large eggs	1⅓ cups diced macadamia nuts
¾ cup sugar	Coconut whipped cream or
1⅓ cups light corn syrup	whipped cream that has been
⅓ cup melted butter	lightly sweetened and flavored
3 tablespoons dark Jamaica rum	with vanilla
1½ teaspoons vanilla	

Beat together until thoroughly mixed the eggs, sugar, syrup, butter, rum, and vanilla. Stir in macadamia nuts. Turn into a buttered 8-inch-square baking pan. Bake in a moderate oven (375°) for 35 to 40 minutes, just until set. Cool on a rack. Spoon into dessert dishes. Top with coconut cream or whipped cream. Makes 8 servings.

Haitian Sweet Potato Pudding (Pain Patate)

¼ cup dark seedless raisins	1 cup firmly packed light brown
3 tablespoons Barbancourt rum	sugar
2 cups finely grated peeled sweet	½ teaspoon ground cinnamon
potatoes	¼ teaspoon salt
⅓ cup grated fresh coconut	⅛ teaspoon freshly ground black
⅔ cup evaporated milk	pepper
½ cup Thick Coconut Milk (see	1½ tablespoons butter
Index)	

2 tablespoons well-mashed ripe | ⅓ cup sifted light brown sugar
banana | Heavy pour cream or softly
½ teaspoon vanilla | whipped cream or warm Rum
1 beaten egg | Raisin Sauce, Haiti (see Index)

Soak raisins in rum for 2 hours. Combine potatoes, coconut, evaporated milk, coconut milk, the 1 cup brown sugar, cinnamon, salt, and pepper in a heavy saucepan. Cook over medium heat, stirring, until potatoes are cooked and mixture is mushy, about 15 minutes. Remove from heat. Add 1 tablespoon of the butter and stir until melted. Allow mixture to cool slightly. Stir in soaked raisins with rum, banana, vanilla, and egg. Turn into a buttered shallow baking dish (about 1 quart). Sprinkle with the sifted brown sugar and dot with the remaining ½ tablespoon butter. Bake in a moderate oven (350°) for 30 minutes or until set. Cool to warm and serve with pour cream or whipped cream. Or cool to room temperature and serve with warm Rum Raisin Sauce, Haiti. Makes 6 servings.

Mexican Cocada, León

1 fresh coconut | 3 tablespoons dark Jamaica rum
1¼ cups sugar | About 3 tablespoons additional
2 cups milk | sugar
4 egg yolks | Toasted almonds

Break open coconut and save the liquid inside. Peel brown skin off coconut meat and grate meat. In a saucepan, combine the coconut liquid and half of the 1¼ cups sugar. Bring to a boil and add grated coconut. Continue to boil gently, stirring, until all of the liquid disappears. Meantime, combine the remaining half of the 1¼ cups sugar and the milk and heat to boiling; pour over coconut. Cook over medium heat, stirring, until mixture cooks down to a thin custard consistency. Remove from heat. Beat egg yolks with rum; very slowly, add to coconut mixture, beating constantly. Return to heat and cook over low heat, stirring, until thickened. Turn into a buttered heatproof platter (so coconut mixture forms a depth of about ½ inch). Sprinkle with the 3 tablespoons sugar. Broil about 6 inches from heat until top is deep golden. Allow to cool to room temperature. Spoon into dessert dishes. Sprinkle with a few almonds. Makes about 16 servings.

Baked Coconut Butter Pudding

½ cup butter	2 cups grated fresh coconut
1 cup sugar	2 tablespoons dark Jamaica rum
3 eggs, separated	¼ teaspoon cream of tartar
1 whole egg	6 tablespoons sugar
2 teaspoons vanilla	

Cream together thoroughly butter and the 1 cup sugar. Beat in the 3 egg yolks and 1 whole egg. Stir in vanilla. Fold in coconut. Turn into a buttered baking dish (about 1½ quarts or 8-inch-square baking pan). Bake in a moderate oven (350°) until toothpick inserted in center comes out clean, about 35 minutes. Sprinkle evenly with rum. Beat egg whites with cream of tartar until foamy. Gradually add the 6 tablespoons of sugar, a tablespoon at a time, beating until whites are stiff and glossy and sugar is dissolved. Pile onto hot pudding and spread to edges. Bake in a hot oven (400°) until lightly browned, about 8 to 10 minutes. Cut into squares or spoon into dessert dishes while warm. Makes 8 servings.

Trinidad Plantation Pudding

Dessert cooks who know rum know that a coffee buttercream is most compatible. Hamish Gordon's Trinidad Plantation Pudding (also called mocha pudding or Alsatian pudding), which he serves in his Barbados Ocean View Hotel dining room, much resembles Madeline's Freezer Cake (see Index). But this hotel dessert is a little more complex than the homemaker's.

This is sheer confection, very rich.

¾ pound soft butter	Medium rum
4 cups sifted powdered sugar	Whipped cream
9 egg yolks	Preserved ginger in syrup,
Rum Coffee Syrup (recipe below)	drained and diced
About 1 pound sponge cake, cut into ½-inch-thick slices	

Cream butter and sugar together thoroughly. Add egg yolks, 1 at a time, and beat until mixture is light and fluffy. Beat in 1 tablespoon of the Rum Coffee Syrup. Line a buttered 10-inch tube cake pan or spring-form pan with waxed paper. Line bottom of pan with cake slices. Spoon on enough of the Rum Coffee Syrup to moisten cake. Spread with a layer of the buttercream. Repeat several times, building alternate layers of cake moistened with syrup and buttercream and ending with cake. Spoon on enough additional rum to moisten all very well, about 4 tablespoons. Cover with waxed paper, then top with a weight. Freeze. At serving time, turn out, remove waxed paper, and decorate with whipped cream and ginger dices. Makes about 20 servings.

RUM COFFEE SYRUP

Stir together 2 tablespoons instant coffee powder (or instant coffee crystals crushed to a powder) and 4 tablespoons water until coffee is dissolved. Stir in 1 cup cream sherry and 4 tablespoons medium rum. Use for Trinidad Plantation Pudding (above).

Jeanne's Persimmon Pudding

One of my daughters, Jeanne Hittell, makes one helluva persimmon pudding. I think that she got started making it years ago when we used to drive up to our ranch through the town of Princeton, California, almost every weekend. On the way, there was a big persimmon tree, and we would watch it all through the early fall, waiting until the persimmons were so ripe that they would fall all over the ground. Then we could buy piles of them from the guy who owned the tree for a buck and a half.

Jeanne likes the pudding with just whipped cream sweetened with sugar and flavored with vanilla. I like it with a bare glaze of the Apricot Rum Sauce and whipped cream or not. Or you can have it with just whipped cream flavored with sugar and a little dark rum.

Just the *littlest* rum accents this. Don't use a lot or you'll kill the pudding taste.

1 cup mashed ripe persimmon pulp	2 teaspoons baking soda
1 cup sugar	½ teaspoon salt
2 tablespoons melted butter	¼ teaspoon ground cinnamon
1 teaspoon vanilla	½ cup milk
1 egg	½ cup moist seedless raisins
1 cup sifted all-purpose flour	½ cup chopped walnuts

Combine in a mixing bowl the persimmon pulp, sugar, butter, vanilla, and egg and beat until smooth. Sift together flour, soda, salt, and cinnamon and slowly beat into persimmon mixture. Beat in milk.

Stir in raisins and walnuts. Pour into a well-buttered 5-cup mold. Cover tightly. Place on a rack over boiling water in covered kettle and let steam for 2 hours. Let cool in mold for 10 minutes. Gently loosen at edges and turn out of mold. Serve while warm. Makes 8 to 12 servings.

APRICOT RUM SAUCE

Slowly heat 1 cup apricot jam to melt it. Remove from heat and stir in 3 tablespoons dark Jamaica rum. Serve with Jeanne's Persimmon Pudding (above). Makes about 1 cup.

PIE AND CANDY

Trader Vic's Nut Rum Pie

If there is anything I love, it's pecan pie. It just drives me out of my cotton-pickin' mind. When you add a little heavy Jamaica rum and some dates, it makes it oh-so-good-peachy.

3 extra-large eggs	¾ cup cut-up moist dates
½ cup sugar	Unbaked pastry for single-crust
1 cup light corn syrup	8-inch pie
¼ cup melted lightly salted butter	Rich vanilla ice cream or
2 tablespoons dark Jamaica rum	whipped cream lightly
1 teaspoon vanilla	sweetened and flavored with
¾ cup chopped pecans	vanilla (optional)

Beat together until thoroughly mixed the eggs, sugar, syrup, butter, rum, and vanilla. Stir in nuts and dates. Turn into pastry-lined 8-inch pie pan. Bake in a moderate oven (375°) for 38 to 40 minutes or until filling is set. Cool on a rack. Serve with ice cream or whipped cream if you wish. Makes 8 servings.

Rum Fudge

Make chocolate fudge according to your favorite recipe *except* flavor with dark Jamaica rum instead of vanilla.

Rum White Fudge

2½ cups sugar
½ cup commercial sour cream
¼ cup milk
2 tablespoons butter
1 tablespoon light corn syrup
⅛ teaspoon salt

1 tablespoon dark Jamaica rum
½ teaspoon vanilla
1 cup roasted and salted
   macadamia nuts, coarsely
   chopped

Combine sugar, sour cream, milk, butter, syrup, and salt in a heavy, deep saucepan. Cook and stir over medium heat until mixture boils and sugar dissolves. Continue to boil without stirring over medium heat until mixture reaches soft ball stage (238° F. on a candy thermometer). Remove from heat and allow to stand until lukewarm (120°), about 1 hour. Add rum and vanilla and beat with a spoon *just* until mixture begins to lose its gloss. Quickly stir in macadamias, turn into a buttered 8-inch-square baking pan (or equivalent shallow platter), and spread smooth. When firm, cut into small squares. Makes 3 dozen pieces. NOTE: Make this fudge on a clear day if possible. If you must make it on a damp day, cook it to 240° instead of 238°.

*So much for the great food;
now for the really great drinks.*

RUM DRINKING

Rum drinking in the States is not what it could be. We just haven't gotten around to drinking very much rum. And I think one main reason is that most people do not know the vast spectrum that rum offers in different tastes, bodies, and aromas. They have experimented with only one or two kinds of rum. They drink a light rum and think it is too mild. They taste a dark Jamaica and think it is too heavy. They don't know that there are rums that are feather light or silky or rich or pungent or full or sweet or fruity or perfumy or clear or dry. . . . (And they have found that Bourbon or scotch or gin tastes pretty much the same, time after time. So they stick with those same tastes all the time.)

Anyone who wants to drink rum and enjoy it should experiment with it. You have to get to know the basic rum qualities and which rums have which qualities. Then you can choose the rum that suits the drink you are going to make—and your tastes—or you can blend rums to suit the drink and your tastes.

Now, you say, but that means I have to get three or four bottles of rum to start with. Sure you do. But that isn't too much to do if you want to have a thing with good taste and enjoyment.

Right now, I am on a kick of drinking Mai Tai Rum Old-fashioneds. This drink is just a regular old-fashioned, but made with our Trader Vic Mai Tai rum instead of Bourbon. I like it because the rum in it is a combination of three or four kinds of rum, blended by me to suit myself. You can do the same thing to suit yourself.

For example, after you know your rums and know what you are doing: Start out with a couple of rums and with the thought that rum is many things, not one thing. And think of getting more than one flavor in your rum drinks. If a drink calls for dark Jamaica rum and you know that you don't want a strong dark flavor, then take some light Puerto Rican rum and mix it into some dark Jamaica rum until you have the flavor that you like. Or sometime you might feel like having a frozen daiquiri made with a richer rum than the light Puerto Rican called for—maybe a Barbancourt 5-star. Go right ahead. This is how you are really going to suit yourself.

But before you have the experience to know your rums, your best bet is to stick to the formulas as they are laid down on these pages. This is true if you want to make good drinks of any kind: Follow the formula, because the formula is the best way to make the drink unless you know that you personally like it a little differently.

And if a formula calls for a particular rum, try to use that rum. For example, if a drink formula calls for Haitian rum, it does so because

Haitian-type rum is important for that particular drink. Haitian is a brandy-type rum and the finest out of the Caribbean.

Many drink formulas in this book do not call for specific brands or types of rums. They merely call for a rum of a general category, as light Puerto Rican or dark Jamaican. In those cases, any good-quality brand of rum within the category is all right to use.

As a general rule, the dark rums, heavy-bodied and full-flavored, are used where the definite flavor of rum is desired—in punches, in hot drinks, or in combination with other rums and liqueurs and fruits. The lighter rums are usually mixed less. In fact, the lighter the rum, the less you mix with it; for the flavor of the rum itself is delicate and should not be killed with strong-flavored ingredients.

But remember that once you get to know your rums and understand their flavors, you don't always have to stick to the book so closely. You can monkey around and blend rums to suit yourself.

Rums for Your Cupboard

If you stock these five rums, you'll be pretty well set up to make almost any rum drink that you'd want to mix—unless you're going to get super-fancy. (If you're going to make Mai Tais or Mai Tai Rum Old-fashioneds, add Trader Vic's Mai Tai rum.)

1. A light Puerto Rican rum (white or light golden) such as Don Q, Ronrico, or Trader Vic's

2. A flavorful golden rum such as Appleton Special from Jamaica, Siegert's Bouquet from Trinidad, or Mount Gay Eclipse from Barbados

3. A smooth, unctuous Haitian Rhum Barbancourt (3-star or 5-star)

4. A Demerara such as Lemon Hart

5. A dark Jamaica such as Myers's Lemon Hart, or Trader Vic's

Simple Syrup

Rock candy syrup is Trader Vic's simple syrup. It is sold in liquor and grocery stores. It is the simple syrup used in all Trader Vic bars.

To make your own simple syrup (sometimes called bar syrup, sugar syrup, or rock candy syrup): Combine 2 pounds granulated sugar and 2 cups water. Boil until sugar is thoroughly dissolved. Cool.

Basic Bar Measurements

Jigger	Usually 1 ounce
Teaspoon or barspoon	⅛ ounce
Dash (as of simple syrup, orgeat, grenadine, lemon juice)	¼ ounce
Dash (as of bitters)	⅛ teaspoon
Scoop (of ice)	About 1 cup
Juice of 1 average lime	1 ounce
Juice of 1 average lemon	1½ ounces

Styles of Drinking

At this point in time, Americans (who know rum at all) tend to know rum best in mixed drinks. But in the rum-producing countries the people, who really know their rums and drink rum with a very sharp sense of the taste of it, tend to drink their favorite rum very simply to taste it very fully—with water, with soda, on the rocks, or neat. Now and then they allow subtle variations on the theme. In Martinique, for example, the real local drink is petit punch—cane syrup, rum, and lime. In Trinidad, where Angostura bitters come from, they dash a bit of Angostura into their rum and add water or soda or whatever; sometimes they even put together a mixed rum drink—a real planter's punch of rum, sugar, lime juice, ice, and Angostura.

Mainly, though, where rum is known, it is exposed. Americans may come to join the drinking styles of the rum countries as they get to know rums better.

As I write this book, I am thinking about food and drinks and wine. For a long time, I felt the same as a lot of other people do: If you have a little rum before dinner and two or three glasses of wine with dinner, your head is going to fall off. Well, I found out differently: If you drink Bourbon or scotch or gin before a load of wine, your head *will* fall off, but if you drink rum first, your head won't roll so far. That's my philosophy.

Trader Vic Rum Drinks

On the following pages original rum drinks by Trader Vic are marked with this motif:

·COCKTAILS·

Adiós Amigos Cocktail

1 ounce light Puerto Rican rum   **½ ounce gin**
½ ounce dry vermouth   **Juice of ½ lime**
½ ounce brandy

Shake with ice cubes. Strain into a large chilled cocktail glass.

Airmail Cocktail

1½ ounces Siegert's Bouquet or   **Juice of ½ lime**
other medium-bodied golden   **1 teaspoon honey**
rum   **Champagne**

Shake rum, lime juice, and honey with ice cubes. Strain into an 8-ounce glass. Fill with champagne. Stir slightly.

Appleton Glow

1½ ounces Appleton Special or   **½ ounce orange juice**
White rum   **1 dash lime juice**
½ ounce Simple Syrup (see
Index)

Shake with ice cubes. Strain into a large chilled cockatil glass. Decorate with a maraschino cherry and a half slice of orange.

Antilles

2 ounces light Puerto Rican rum
½ ounce blond Dubonnet

Stir with ice cubes to blend. Strain into a chilled cocktail glass. Twist orange peel over drink.

Antoine's Lullaby

4 ounces light Puerto Rican rum   **¼ ounce Grand Marnier**
1 ounce red Dubonnet   **¾ ounce lemon juice**

Stir with ice in a pitcher or mixing glass. Strain into 4 chilled cocktail glasses with sugar-frosted rims.

Arawak Cocktail

1½ ounces Jamaica rum   1 dash Angostura bitters
1½ ounces sweet sherry

Stir in a mixing glass with ice cubes. Strain into a chilled cocktail glass.

Bacardi Cocktail

1 ounce Bacardi light Puerto   1 dash grenadine
  Rican rum   Juice of 1 lime

Shake with ice cubes. Strain into a chilled tiki stem cocktail glass or small pilsner glass or cocktail glass.

Barbados Cocktail

1 ounce Barbados rum   1 dash rock candy syrup
1 dash maraschino liqueur   Juice of 1 lime

Shake with ice cubes. Strain into a chilled tiki stem cocktail glass. Decorate with a thin lime slice.

Barbancourt Stir

1 ounce Barbancourt 5-star rum   ⅓ ounce Grand Marnier
⅓ ounce sweet vermouth

Stir with shaved ice. Pour into a chilled cocktail glass. Decorate with a lime slice.

Barbancourt Zoom

1½ ounces Barbancourt 5-star   1 teaspoon honey
  rum   2 teaspoons fresh heavy cream

Shake well in an electric drink mixer (or in a shaker can with mixing glass) with ice cubes. Strain into a chilled cocktail glass.

Beige Cocktail

¼ ounce dark Jamaica rum   ½ ounce heavy cream
1 ounce Kahlúa

Blend with shaved ice in an electric drink mixer. Strain into a chilled cocktail glass.

Black Widow

1 ounce Barbados rum   1 dash Simple Syrup (see Index)
½ ounce Southern Comfort   Juice of ½ lime

Shake with ice cubes. Strain into a chilled tiki stem (or other) cocktail glass.

Bulldog Cocktail

¾ ounce light Puerto Rican rum   Juice of ½ lime
1½ ounces cherry brandy

Shake with ice cubes. Strain into a chilled double cocktail glass.

California Street Cocktail

1 fresh pineapple stick   Juice of ½ lime
2 ounces light Puerto Rican rum   1 teaspoon bar sugar

Fill an old-fashioned glass with ice cubes. Rub rim of the glass with a stick of fresh pineapple. Shake rum, lime juice, and sugar with ice cubes. Strain into the prepared glass.

Caribe Cocktail

1½ ounces light Puerto Rican   ¾ ounce lemon juice
   rum   1 ounce pineapple juice

Shake with ice cubes. Strain into a chilled cocktail glass.

Champs-de-Mars Daiquiri

2 ounces Barbancourt 5-star rum   1 teaspoon grenadine
1 teaspoon maraschino liqueur   Juice of ½ lime

Shake well with ice cubes. Strain into a chilled cocktail glass.

Chinese Cocktail

1 ounce Jamaica rum   1 dash curaçao
1 dash Angostura bitters   1 teaspoon grenadine
1 dash maraschino liqueur

Stir well with ice cubes. Strain into a chilled cocktail glass. Twist lemon peel over drink. Add a maraschino cherry.

Coctel Veracruzana

1 ounce dark Jamaica rum   1 ounce pineapple juice
1 ounce dry vermouth

Shake well with ice cubes. Strain into a chilled cocktail glass.

Cointreau Cocktail

½ ounce light Puerto Rican rum   ½ ounce gin
½ ounce Cointreau

Shake with ice cubes. Strain into a chilled cocktail glass.

Columbus Cocktail

1 ounce Barbancourt 5-star or   1 ounce apricot brandy
  Barbados rum   1 ounce lime juice

Shake with ice cubes. Strain into a chilled cocktail glass.

Coquetail au Vanilla

1 vanilla bean, split lengthwise   Falernum
1 fifth Barbancourt 5-star rum   Lime slices

Add vanilla bean to bottle of rum, cover, and chill for 24 hours. For each drink: Fill a champagne glass with shaved ice and add 1 teaspoon Falernum and a thin lime slice. Fill with vanilla rum. Makes about 30 servings.

Cream of Coconut Cocktail (Caneel Bay Plantation)

1 ounce light Virgin Islands rum   **1 ounce evaporated milk**
1 ounce Lopez coconut cream

Shake in a commercial electric drink mixer (or in a shaker can with mixing glass) with ice cubes. Strain into a chilled cocktail glass. Dust with ground cinnamon or grated nutmeg.

Cuba Libre Cocktail

1 ounce light Puerto Rican rum   **Juice of ½ lime**
1 ounce Coca-Cola

Shake with ice cubes. Strain into a chilled cocktail glass.

Cuban Cocktail—1

1 ounce light Puerto Rican rum
½ ounce fresh lime juice

Shake with ice cubes. Strain into a chilled cocktail glass.

Cuban Cocktail—2

1½ ounces light Puerto Rican   **½ teaspoon grenadine**
**   rum**   **1 dash orange bitters**
½ teaspoon maraschino liqueur   **2 drops lemon juice**

Shake with ice cubes. Strain into a chilled cocktail glass. Twist lemon peel over drink.

Cuban Cocktail—3

1 teaspoon Jamaica rum   **1½ ounces brandy**
½ ounce apricot brandy   **Juice of ½ lime or ¼ lemon**

Shake with ice cubes. Strain into a chilled cocktail glass.

Cuban Presidente

1 ounce light Puerto Rican or
   Cuban rum
1 dash curaçao

1 dash grenadine
½ ounce dry vermouth
Juice of ½ lime

Shake with ice cubes. Strain into a tiki stem or other cocktail glass. Add a twist of orange peel.

Daiquiri Cocktail

1 ounce light Puerto Rican rum
1 dash maraschino liqueur

1 dash Simple Syrup (see Index)
Juice of 1 lime

Shake with ice cubes. Strain into a chilled tiki stem or other large cocktail glass. Decorate with a thin lime slice.

Del Monte Cocktail

1½ ounces light Puerto Rican
   rum

½ teaspoon grenadine
½ teaspoon lemon juice

Shake with ice cubes. Strain into a chilled cocktail glass.

Drinker's Delight

1½ ounces light Puerto Rican
   rum
½ teaspoon curaçao

½ teaspoon grenadine
1 egg white
1 teaspoon pineapple juice

Shake with ice cubes. Strain into a chilled cocktail glass.

El Presidente

1 ounce light Puerto Rican rum
½ ounce dry vermouth

1 teaspoon grenadine
1 dash curaçao

Stir with ice cubes. Strain into a chilled cocktail glass.

Eye-opener

1 ounce Barbancourt 5-star rum	2 dashes orgeat syrup
½ ounce Grand Marnier	1 egg yolk

Shake well with ice cubes. Strain into a chilled cocktail glass. VARIATION: Add 1 dash lime juice.

Far East Cocktail

1 teaspoon curaçao	1½ ounces dark Jamaica rum
3 dashes grenadine	1 dash Angostura bitters

Shake with ice cubes. Strain into a chilled cocktail glass. Add a maraschino cherry.

Fiesta Cocktail

1½ ounces light Puerto Rican rum	½ ounce calvados or applejack
	½ ounce dry vermouth

Shake with ice cubes. Strain into a chilled cocktail glass.

Fruiteer

1 ounce dark New England or Jamaica rum	¼ ounce lime or lemon juice
¾ ounce sweetened raspberry or loganberry juice	1 teaspoon Benedictine

Shake with ice cubes. Strain into a chilled cocktail glass.

Haitian Club

1 ounce Barbancourt 5-star rum
½ ounce dry vermouth

Shake with ice cubes. Strain into a chilled cocktail glass. Add a cocktail olive if you wish.

Havana Beach Cocktail

1 ounce light Puerto Rican or　　**1 ounce pineapple juice**
　Cuban rum　　　　　　　　　**1 teaspoon sugar**

Shake with ice cubes. Strain into a large chilled cocktail glass.

Havana Cocktail

1½ ounces sweet sherry　　　**1 teaspoon lemon juice**
1½ ounces white Puerto Rican or
　Cuban rum

Shake with ice cubes. Strain into a chilled cocktail glass.

Hawaiian Cocktail

1½ ounces Barbancourt 5-star or　**1 dash orange bitters**
　Barbados rum　　　　　　　　　**1 egg white**
1½ ounces pineapple juice

Shake with ice cubes. Strain into a large chilled cocktail glass.

Hibiscus

1½ ounces light Puerto Rican　　**1 teaspoon grenadine**
　rum　　　　　　　　　　　　**Juice of ¼ lemon**
1 teaspoon dry vermouth

Shake with ice cubes. Strain into a chilled cocktail glass.

Honeysuckle

1½ ounces Barbancourt 5-star or　**1 teaspoon honey**
　Barbados rum　　　　　　　　**Juice of 1 lime or ½ lemon**

Shake well with ice cubes. Strain into a chilled cocktail glass.

Huapala Cocktail

¾ ounce light Puerto Rican rum　**1 dash grenadine**
¾ ounce gin　　　　　　　　　**½ ounce lemon juice**

Shake with ice cubes. Strain into a chilled cocktail glass.

Ibo Lele Cocktail

2 ounces Barbancourt 5-star rum
½ ounce Dubonnet or port
Juice of 1 lime
½ ounce grenadine or Simple
  Syrup (see Index)
1 dash Angostura bitters

Shake with ice cubes. Strain into a chilled cocktail glass. Decorate with a maraschino cherry.

Jamaica Honey Bee

1 tablespoon honey
½ ounce lemon juice
2 ounces dark Jamaica rum

In a mixing glass, stir honey and lemon juice to blend. Add ice cubes and rum. Shake. Strain into a chilled large cocktail glass.

Jamaica Rum Cocktail

2 ounces dark Jamaica rum
1 teaspoon bar sugar
Juice of ½ lime

Shake with ice cubes. Strain into a chilled cocktail glass.

Knickerbocker Special Cocktail

2 ounces light Puerto Rican rum
½ teaspoon curaçao
1 teaspoon raspberry syrup
1 teaspoon lemon juice
1 teaspoon orange juice

Shake with ice cubes. Strain into a chilled 4-ounce cocktail glass. Decorate with a small slice of pineapple.

La Florida Cocktail

1 ounce light Puerto Rican rum
½ ounce sweet vermouth
1 dash grenadine
1 dash curaçao
¼ ounce crème de cacao
Juice of 1 lime

Shake with ice cubes. Strain into a chilled tiki stem champagne glass or other large saucer champagne glass. Add a twist of orange peel.

Lanai Cocktail

½ cup light Puerto Rican rum   1 teaspoon lime juice
1 cup pineapple juice

Mix in an electric drink mixer with ice cubes. Strain into 3 chilled champagne glasses.

L'International

½ ounce light Puerto Rican rum   ½ ounce gin
½ ounce dry vermouth   2 dashes pineapple juice

Shake with ice cubes. Strain into a chilled cocktail glass.

Lisbon Antigua

1¼ jiggers Barbancourt 5-star or   ¾ jigger white port
  Barbados rum   1 dash Angostura bitters

Shake with ice cubes. Strain into a chilled cocktail glass. Add a maraschino cherry and a small orange slice.

Mambo

Because bottled cranberry juices vary in sweetness, you may need to sweeten this to taste.

1 ounce dark Jamaica rum
3 ounces cranberry juice

Stir with ice cubes. Strain into a large chilled cocktail glass.

Mary Pickford Cocktail

There are many versions of this old-time cocktail. You can step up the rum to 2 ounces and reduce the pineapple juice to ¾ ounce, for example.

1½ ounces light Puerto Rican   1 dash maraschino liqueur
  rum   1½ ounces pineapple juice
1 teaspoon grenadine

Shake well with ice cubes. Strain into a chilled cocktail glass.

Millionaire Cocktail—1

½ ounce light Jamaica rum
½ ounce apricot brandy
½ ounce sloe gin

1 dash grenadine
Juice of 1 lime

Shake with ice cubes. Strain into a chilled cocktail glass.

Millionaire Cocktail—2

½ ounce light Jamaica rum
1½ ounces sloe gin

½ ounce apricot brandy
1 dash grenadine

Shake with ice cubes. Strain into a chilled cocktail glass.

Montego Bay Cocktail

1 ounce Rhum Negrita
Juice of ½ lime
1 dash rock candy syrup

1 dash Triple Sec
1 dash Angostura bitters

Shake with ice cubes. Strain into a chilled tiki stem cocktail glass.

Naked Lady

½ ounce Barbancourt 5-star rum
½ ounce sweet vermouth
1 ounce apricot liqueur

2 dashes grenadine
Juice of ½ lemon

Shake with ice cubes. Strain into a chilled cocktail glass.

Orange Daiquiri

1½ ounces light Puerto Rican
   rum
1 ounce orange juice

½ ounce lime juice
½ ounce Simple Syrup (see
   Index)

Blend with 1 scoop shaved ice for 10 to 20 seconds in an electric drink mixer. Pour into a chilled cocktail glass.

Palmetto Cocktail

1¼ ounces light Puerto Rican rum	1¼ ounces dry vermouth
	2 dashes Angostura bitters

Stir with ice cubes. Strain into a chilled cocktail glass.

Pancho Villa Cocktail

1 ounce light Puerto Rican rum	1 teaspoon cherry brandy
1 ounce apricot brandy	1 teaspoon pineapple juice
1 ounce gin	

Shake well with shaved ice and strain into a chilled champagne glass.

Passion Daiquiri Cocktail

1½ ounces light Puerto Rican rum	1 teaspoon bar sugar
	½ ounce passion fruit nectar
Juice of 1 lime	

Shake with ice cubes. Strain into a chilled cocktail glass.

Plantation Cocktail

1 ounce dark Jamaica rum	½ ounce orange juice
½ ounce lemon juice	

Shake with ice cubes. Strain into a chilled cocktail glass.

Planter's Cocktail—1

1 ounce light Puerto Rican rum	1 dash lemon juice
1 ounce orange juice	

Shake with ice cubes. Strain into a chilled cocktail glass.

Planter's Cocktail—2

1 ounce dark Jamaica rum	½ teaspoon bar sugar
1 ounce lemon juice	

Shake with ice cubes. Strain into a chilled cocktail glass.

Planter's Cocktail—3

1 ounce Barbancourt 5-star rum   **Juice of ½ lemon**
1 ounce orange juice

Shake with ice cubes. Strain into a chilled champagne glass. Add a twist of lemon peel if you wish.

Platinum Blonde

1 ounce Barbancourt 5-star or   **1 ounce Grand Marnier**
** Barbados rum**   **½ ounce fresh cream**

Shake with ice cubes. Strain into a chilled cocktail glass.

Port-au-Prince

1 ounce Barbancourt 5-star rum   **Juice of ½ lime**
½ ounce crème de cassis

Shake with ice cubes. Strain into a chilled cocktail glass.

President Cocktail—1

1 ounce light Puerto Rican rum   **½ ounce dry vermouth**
½ ounce curaçao   **1 dash grenadine**

Shake with ice cubes. Strain into a chilled cocktail glass. Add a twist of orange peel.

President Cocktail—2

1½ ounces light Puerto Rican   **2 dashes grenadine**
** rum**   **Juice of ¼ orange**

Shake with ice cubes. Strain into a chilled cocktail glass.

President Cocktail—3

1½ ounces light Puerto Rican
  rum
1 dash grenadine

1 teaspoon orange juice
1 dash lemon juice

Shake well with ice cubes. Strain into a chilled cocktail glass.

President Roosevelt Cocktail

1½ ounces light Puerto Rican
  rum

1 dash grenadine
1 teaspoon orange juice

Shake with ice cubes. Strain into a chilled cocktail glass.

Providence Plantation

1 bottle (fifth) light Puerto Rican
  rum
1 can (1 pint, 2 ounces)
  unsweetened pineapple juice

1½ cups orange juice
1 beaten egg white

Stir well with ice cubes. Strain into chilled cocktail glasses. Makes 8 to 10 servings.

Quarter Deck Cocktail—1

1 ounce light Puerto Rican rum
½ ounce sweet sherry

2 dashes lemon juice

Shake with ice cubes. Strain into a chilled cocktail glass.

Quarter Deck Cocktail—2

1 ounce dark Jamaica rum
½ ounce sweet sherry
½ ounce scotch

1 teaspoon Simple Syrup (see
  Index)
1 dash orange bitters

Shake with ice cubes. Strain into a chilled cocktail glass.

Quarter Deck Cocktail—3

| 1 ounce Barbancourt 5-star or light Puerto Rican rum | ½ ounce sweet sherry
1 teaspoon lime juice |

Shake with ice cubes. Strain into a chilled cocktail glass.

Rocky Mountain Cocktail

| ¾ ounce Trader Vic rum and brandy (or half light Puerto Rican rum and half brandy) | ¾ ounce Bols Crème de Noyaux
Juice of ½ lime |

Shake with ice cubes. Strain into a tiki stem champagne or other saucer champagne glass. Add a few small ice cubes. Decorate with a rock candy stick.

Royal Bermuda Yacht Club Cocktail

| 1½ ounces Barbados rum
¼ ounce Falernum | 1 dash Cointreau
½ ounce lime juice |

Shake with ice cubes. Strain into a chilled cocktail glass.

Rum Cocktail

2 ounces Siegert's Bouquet or other medium-bodied golden rum
2 dashes Angostura bitters

Shake well with ice cubes. Strain into a sour glass.

Rum Dubonnet

½ ounce Barbancourt 5-star rum   1 teaspoon lime juice
½ ounce Dubonnet

Shake with ice cubes. Strain into a chilled cocktail glass.

Rum Gimlet

1½ ounces light Puerto Rican rum
½ ounce Rose's lime juice (sweetened)

Shake with ice cubes. Strain into a chilled cocktail glass. Add a thin slice of lime.

Rum Manhattan

1 ounce Siegert's Bouquet or
   other medium-bodied golden
   rum

½ ounce sweet vermouth
1 dash Angostura bitters

Stir with ice cubes. Strain into a chilled cocktail glass. Add a twist of lemon peel.

Rum Twist

1½ ounces Barbancourt 5-star
   rum
½ ounce lime juice

⅓ ounce orange curaçao
¼ ounce raspberry syrup

Stir well with shaved ice. Strain into a chilled champagne glass. Add a twist of lime peel.

Sec Elite

1 ounce light Puerto Rican rum
¾ ounce dry sherry

¾ ounce blond Dubonnet
1 dash Pernod or Herbsaint

Shake with ice cubes. Strain into a chilled cocktail glass.

September Morn

1½ ounces light Puerto Rican
   rum
Juice of ¼ lime

Juice of ¼ lemon
1 teaspoon brown sugar
1 egg white

Shake well with ice cubes. Strain into a chilled cocktail glass.

Shanghai Cocktail

1 ounce dark Jamaica rum
1 teaspoon anisette

½ teaspoon grenadine
Juice of ¼ lemon

Shake with ice cubes. Strain into a chilled cocktail glass.

Siegert's Bouquet Cocktail

We made up this cocktail years ago. It is such a nice cocktail.

1 ounce Siegert's Bouquet rum   ½ ounce lemon juice
¼ ounce orgeat syrup

Shake with ice cubes. Strain into a chilled tiki stem or other cocktail glass.

Sir Walter Cocktail

¾ ounce light Puerto Rican rum   1 teaspoon curaçao
¾ ounce brandy   1 teaspoon lemon juice
1 teaspoon grenadine

Shake with ice cubes. Strain into a chilled cocktail glass.

Tabu Cocktail

1½ ounces light Puerto Rican   1 slice pineapple
   rum   ½ ounce cranberry syrup
1 scant teaspoon bar sugar   ½ ounce lemon juice

Blend in an electric drink mixer with ½ scoop shaved ice. Pour into a large chilled champagne glass.

Tahitian Honey Bee

½ ounce lemon juice   1½ ounces light Puerto Rican
1 teaspoon honey   rum

Mix lemon juice and honey in a shaker. Add rum. Shake with ice cubes. Strain into a chilled cocktail glass. Add a twist of lemon peel. VARIATION: Increase rum to 2 ounces and honey to 2 teaspoons.

Trader Vic Cocktail

1 ounce Siegert's Bouquet rum   1 dash rock candy syrup
Juice of ½ lime

Shake with ice cubes. Strain into a chilled tiki stem cocktail or other cocktail glass.

Tropical Cocktail

2 slices fresh pineapple
Sugar
Juice of 1 lime

2 dashes Simple Syrup (see Index)
1½ ounces dark Jamaica rum

Sprinkle pineapple with sugar to taste. Crush well. Put into an electric drink mixer along with lime juice, syrup, rum, and ice cubes. Shake well. Strain into a chilled wine glass.

Acapulco Gold

If you don't have the coconut cream, leave it out. It's still a pretty good drink.

1 ounce Jamaica rum	½ ounce frozen concentrated
1 ounce tequila	grapefruit juice (undiluted)
2 ounces pineapple juice	1 ounce Lopez coconut cream

Shake well with ice cubes. Strain into a tall chimney glass over ice cubes.

Aku Aku

1 ounce light Puerto Rican rum	8 or 10 large fresh mint leaves
½ ounce peach liqueur	1 dash rock candy syrup
Juice of 1 lime	½ slice pineapple

Blend thoroughly with a 12-ounce glass of shaved ice in an electric drink mixer. Serve in a tiki stem pearl glass or large cocktail glass.

Añejo Daiquiri

1 ounce Bacardi Añejo rum	Juice of 1 lime
1 dash maraschino liqueur	1 dash Simple Syrup (see Index)

Blend with 1 scoop shaved ice in an electric drink mixer. Strain through a medium-mesh kitchen strainer into a chilled saucer champagne glass.

Apricot Lady

2 ounces Barbancourt 5-star rum	3 ounces apricot juice (nectar)
½ ounce curaçao	1 egg white

Blend with ½ scoop shaved ice in an electric drink mixer. Pour into a chilled 10- or 12-ounce fizz glass or footed iced tea glass.

Around the World

3 ounces light Puerto Rican rum	3 ounces lemon juice
½ ounce brandy	1 ounce orgeat syrup
3 ounces orange juice	Juice of ½ lime

Blend with 2 scoops of shaved ice for 12 to 15 seconds in an electric drink mixer. Pour into 2 large-bowled goblets. Fill glasses with cracked ice. Serve with straws.

Aunt Agatha

1½ ounces light Puerto Rican rum	2 ounces orange juice
rum	Angostura bitters

Pour rum and orange juice over ice cubes in an old-fashioned glass. Stir. Float a few drops of bitters on top. VARIATION: Substitute grapefruit juice for orange juice.

Babalu

2 ounces golden Puerto Rican rum	½ ounce lemon juice
rum	¼ ounce rock candy syrup
¾ ounce frozen concentrated pineapple-grapefruit juice (undiluted)	

Blend with 1 scoop shaved ice in an electric drink mixer. Serve in a voodoo glass or tall tumbler with cracked ice. Decorate with fresh mint and a fruit stick.

Bahia

1 ounce white Jamaica rum	1 ounce Lopez coconut cream
1 ounce light Puerto Rican rum	
2½ ounces unsweetened	
pineapple juice	

Mix with ice cubes in a commercial electric drink mixer (or by hand with a shaker can and, mixing glass). Pour into a 10-ounce pilsner glass. Fill with cracked ice. Decorate with fresh mint and a fruit stick.

Banana Daiquiri

1 ounce light Puerto Rican rum	1 teaspoon bar sugar
1 dash maraschino liqueur	1 1-inch slice of banana
Juice of 1 lime	

Blend with 1 scoop shaved ice in an electric drink mixer. Strain through a medium-mesh kitchen strainer into a chilled tiki stem champagne glass or 4½-ounce champagne glass.

Banana Jumbie (Buccaneer Hotel, St. Croix)

151-proof Virgin Islands rum	1 teaspoon sugar
¾ ounce banana liqueur	1 peeled ripe banana
1 ounce lime juice	

Blend 1½ ounces rum, liqueur, lime juice, sugar, and banana in an electric drink mixer with 1 scoop shaved ice until mixture is the consistency of snow. Pour into a large heatproof bowl-shaped container. Add a float of rum and flame it.

Barbancourt Crusta

1 lemon	2 teaspoons bar sugar
6 ounces Barbancourt 5-star rum	2 dashes Angostura bitters
2 teaspoons maraschino liqueur	

Spiral-cut the peel off the lemon. Cut peel in half; use each half to line the inside of a wine glass. Moisten the edge of each glass and dip into powdered sugar to frost. Squeeze juice from lemon and blend with remaining ingredients and ½ cup crushed ice in an electric drink mixer. Pour into the prepared glasses. Makes 2 drinks.

Barbancourt Rum Old-fashioned

1 small cocktail sugar cube	**Club soda**
1 dash Angostura bitters	**2 ounces Barbancourt 5-star rum**

Put sugar into an old-fashioned glass. Dash bitters onto sugar. Add a splash of soda. Muddle. Add ice cubes, then rum. Stir. Decorate with a slice of orange, a slice of lemon, and a maraschino cherry.

Barbancourt Special

1 rounded teaspoon brown sugar	**1½ ounces grapefruit juice**
2 ounces Barbancourt 5-star rum	

Dissolve sugar in rum. Pour into a double old-fashioned glass filled with ice cubes. Add grapefruit juice. Shake well. Decorate with a fruit stick and a mint sprig.

Beachcomber

2 ounces light Puerto Rican rum	**2 dashes maraschino liqueur**
½ ounce Cointreau	**Juice of ½ lime**

Blend with shaved ice in an electric drink mixer. Pour, unstrained, into a chilled champagne glass.

Big Bamboo

2 ounces Appleton Special or White Jamaica rum	**¼ ounce lime juice**
¼ ounce Triple Sec	**¼ ounce orange juice**
¼ ounce Simple Syrup (see Index)	

Pack a tall mug with shaved ice. Blend all ingredients together in an electric drink mixer. Pour into the prepared mug. Garnish with a mint sprig. Serve with a straw.

Bluebeard's Ghost (Caneel Bay Plantation)

4 ounces light Virgin Islands rum	2 ounces lemon juice
2 ounces orange curaçao	2 ounces Simple Syrup (see Index)
1½ ounces red burgundy	

Shake with ice cubes. Pour, with ice, into 4 tall glasses.

Café San Juan (Cold)

2 ounces golden Puerto Rican rum
Strong cold coffee

Pour rum over ice cubes in a highball glass. Fill with coffee. Stir. Twist lemon peel over drink. If desired, add sugar to taste.

Caravan Special

1½ ounces light Virgin Islands or Puerto Rican rum	1 dash grenadine
½ ounce apricot brandy	2 ounces mixed fruit juices
	1 ounce fresh cream

Shake with ice cubes. Pour into a 12-ounce glass. Decorate with fresh fruit. Sprinkle with grated nutmeg.

Caribe Cresta

When I was writing my Mexican cookbook, I traveled through the Yucatán peninsula to get some recipes for Mexican food; and I liked the place. So when I told Sarvis to go down to the Caribbean, I suggested that she come back through that same part of Mexico. In Cozumel, she met the manageress of the Hotel Cozumel Caribe. This woman came up with a drink that sounds to me as if it would taste like the inside of a motorman's glove. But we tried it and it was good. In Cozumel they like it for a tall afternoon drink while sunning and swimming at the sandy beach.

2 ounces golden Mexican (or
  other golden) rum
1 ounce fresh cream
½ ounce crème de cacao

¼ ounce Simple Syrup (see
  Index)
Coca-Cola

Shake rum, cream, crème de cacao, and syrup with ice cubes. Pour into a 14-ounce chimney glass. Fill with Coca-Cola. Stir. Dust with grated fresh nutmeg. Serve with a straw.

Carnival Jump Up (Trinidad Hilton)

2 ounces golden Trinidad rum
½ ounce grenadine

1 ounce Lopez coconut cream
½ ounce lime juice

Shake with ice cubes. Pour, with ice, into a tall highball glass. Decorate with a fresh pineapple slice, a candy sugarcane stick, and a lime slice. Serve with a straw.

Chinese Itch

1 ounce golden Puerto Rican rum
Juice of 1 lime

¾ ounce passion fruit nectar
1 dash orgeat syrup

Shake well in a commercial drink mixer (or in a shaker can with mixing glass) with ice cubes. Strain into a tiki stem or other large saucer champagne glass.

Clipper

1 ounce light Puerto Rican rum
1 ounce gin
1 dash grenadine
1 dash Pernod or Herbsaint

1 ounce lime juice
1 teaspoon bar sugar
Club soda

Shake all ingredients except soda with ice cubes. Strain into a 12-ounce chimney glass. Fill glass with chilled soda. Decorate with a fruit stick and a mint sprig.

Coco Loco

1½ ounces light Virgin Islands
  rum
2 ounces Lopez coconut cream

1 cup crushed pineapple
½ ounce lemon juice

Blend with 1 small scoop shaved ice in an electric drink mixer until mixture is foamy. Pour into a fresh coconut shell or a 10-ounce glass.

Coconut Daiquiri

1 ounce light Puerto Rican rum   **Juice of 1 lime**
1½ tablespoons Lopez coconut
  cream

Blend with 1 small scoop shaved ice in an electric drink mixer. Strain through a medium-mesh kitchen strainer into a chilled 4½-ounce champagne glass.

Coffee Frosted

2 ounces Barbancourt 5-star rum   **1 tablespoon bar sugar**
2 ounces cool strong coffee   **1 dash ground cloves**

Blend with ½ scoop shaved ice in an electric drink mixer. Pour into a chilled 8-ounce glass.

Cruzan Confusion (Buccaneer Hotel)

1¼ ounces light Virgin Islands   **1¼ ounces lime juice**
  rum   **¼ ounce Lopez coconut cream**
1¼ ounces tequila   **151-proof Virgin Islands rum**
¼ ounce Benedictine

Blend light rum, tequila, Benedictine, lime juice, and coconut cream in an electric drink mixer with 1 scoop shaved ice. Pour into a double old-fashioned glass. Add a float of 151-proof rum.

Cuba Libre—1

½ fresh lime   **Coca-Cola**
1 ounce light Puerto Rican rum

Squeeze lime juice into a 12-ounce highball glass ¾ filled with ice cubes; save shell. Add rum. Add Coca-Cola to fill ¾ full. Stir lightly. Add the spent lime shell.

Cuba Libre—2

1 lime	**Coca-Cola**
2 ounces light Puerto Rican rum	

Cut lime and squeeze juice into highball glass, dropping in shells. Muddle lime shells. Add ice cubes to nearly fill. Add rum. Stir. Fill with Coca-Cola.

Daiquiri (frozen)—1

2 ounces light Puerto Rican rum	**Juice of ½ lime**
1 dash maraschino liqueur	**1 teaspoon bar sugar**

Blend with ½ scoop shaved ice in an electric drink mixer. Pour into a chilled champagne glass.

Daiquiri (frozen)—2

1 ounce light Puerto Rican rum	**1 dash Simple Syrup (see Index)**
Juice of 1 lime	**or grenadine**

Blend with 10 ounces shaved ice in an electric drink mixer. Pile up in a chilled champagne glass. Serve with a short straw.

Daiquiri Collins

2 ounces light Puerto Rican rum	**1 teaspoon bar sugar**
1 ounce fresh lime juice	**Club soda**

Pour rum, lime juice, and sugar over ice cubes in a highball glass. Fill glass with soda. Stir gently.

Daiquiri on the Rocks

2 ounces light Puerto Rican rum	**Juice of 1 lime**
½ ounce maraschino liqueur	**1 dash Simple Syrup (see Index)**

Pour over ice cubes in an old-fashioned glass. Stir.

Daiquiris by the Pitcher

12 ounces light Puerto Rican rum   **6 ounces ice water**
1 6-ounce can frozen daiquiri
  mix, thawed

Half fill a 2-quart pitcher with ice cubes. Pour in rum, daiquiri mix, and water. Stir well. Strain into cocktail glasses or pour over ice cubes in old-fashioned glasses. Makes 8 drinks.

Daiquiris by Two

6 ounces Barbancourt 5-star rum   **Juice of 1 lime**
½ ounce grenadine or Simple
  Syrup (see Index)

Blend in an electric drink mixer with ½ cup shaved ice. Strain into 2 chilled cocktail glasses.

Demerara Dry Float

1 ounce 86-proof Demerara rum   **1 dash rock candy syrup**
1 dash maraschino liqueur   **1 dash lemon juice**
Juice of 1 lime   **¼ ounce 151-proof Demerara**
½ ounce passion fruit nectar   **rum**

Shake well all ingredients except 151-proof rum in a commercial electric drink mixer (or in a shaker can with mixing glass) with ice cubes. Strain into a footed ice tea or 10-ounce glass. Float the 151-proof Demerara.

Dr. Funk

I didn't originate this drink, but it is as close as I can come to matching the original.

½ lime   **2 ounces dark Jamaica or**
½ ounce lemon juice   **Martinique rum**
1 dash grenadine   **2 ounces club soda**
1 dash Simple Syrup (see Index)   **1 dash Pernod or Herbsaint**

Squeeze lime juice into a mixing glass with ice cubes; save shell. Add lemon juice, grenadine, syrup, rum, and soda. Stir well. Strain into a 14-ounce chimney glass filled with ice cubes. Float Pernod or Herbsaint. Decorate with a fresh mint sprig and the spent lime shell.

Dr. Funk's Son

This is the drink that I originated, and I think that it's better than Dr. Funk.

½ lime	½ ounce lemon juice
½ ounce Ron Rico purple label 151-proof rum	1 dash grenadine
	1 dash rock candy syrup
2 ounces dark Jamaica rum	2 ounces club soda

Squeeze lime juice into a mixing glass with ice cubes; save shell. Add remaining ingredients; stir well. Pour into a 12-ounce glass. Decorate with fresh mint, the spent lime shell, and a fruit stick.

Dudley Darbury

1½ ounces light Puerto Rican rum	Juice of ½ lemon
	Juice of ⅓ orange
½ ounce Triple Sec	Club soda

Shake rum, Triple Sec, and lemon and orange juices with ice cubes. Strain into a 10-ounce glass filled with 3 ice cubes. Add chilled soda to fill glass. Garnish with a lime slice, a maraschino cherry, and a sprig of mint.

Fireman's Sour

½ ounce grenadine	Juice of 1 lime
½ teaspoon bar sugar	Club soda
2 ounces light Puerto Rican rum	

Shake grenadine, sugar, rum, and lime juice with ice cubes. Strain into a sour glass. Fill glass with soda. Decorate with a slice of orange and a maraschino cherry.

Floridita Daiquiri

1½ ounces light Puerto Rican rum	¼ ounce grapefruit juice
	½ ounce lime juice
½ teaspoon maraschino liqueur	1 teaspoon bar sugar

Blend with 1 scoop shaved ice for 10 to 20 seconds in an electric drink mixer. Pour, unstrained, into a large cocktail glass.

Fog Cutter

2 ounces light Puerto Rican rum	**1 ounce orange juice**
1 ounce brandy	**½ ounce orgeat syrup**
½ ounce gin	**Sweet sherry**
2 ounces lemon juice	

Shake all ingredients except sherry with ice cubes. Pour into a 14-ounce glass. Add more ice cubes. Add a sherry float. Serve with straws.

Foul Weather

1 ounce dark Jamaica rum	**½ ounce passion fruit nectar**
1 ounce light Puerto Rican rum	**1 dash vanilla**
1 ounce orange juice	**1 dash Simple Syrup (see Index)**
1 ounce lemon juice	

Pour over ice in a tall highball glass. Stir well. Decorate with fresh mint and a fruit stick.

Frozen Mint Daiquiri

2 ounces light Puerto Rican rum	**1 ounce lime juice**
1 ounce white crème de menthe	

Blend in an electric drink mixer with ½ scoop shaved ice for about 15 seconds. Pour into a chilled champagne saucer.

Frozen Peach Daiquiri

1½ ounces light Puerto Rican rum	**Juice of ½ lime**
2 dashes curaçao	**½ teaspoon bar sugar**
	½ fresh ripe freestone peach

Blend in an electric drink mixer with ½ scoop shaved ice. Pour into a chilled champagne glass. VARIATION: Substitute several large ripe strawberries for the peach.

Havana Gold

1 ounce light Puerto Rican rum	Juice of 1 lime
1 dash Herbsaint	1 teaspoon bar sugar
1 dash maraschino liqueur	

Blend with 1 scoop shaved ice in an electric drink mixer. Strain through a medium-mesh kitchen strainer into a tiki stem or other large saucer champagne glass.

Honolulu

1½ ounces light Puerto Rican rum	½ slice pineapple
1 dash grenadine	½ ounce lemon juice
	1 dash rock candy syrup

Blend with a 12-ounce glass of shaved ice in an electric drink mixer. Strain through a medium-mesh kitchen strainer into a tiki stem champagne compote or other 10-ounce champagne compote.

Hurricane Buster

1½ ounces light Virgin Islands or Puerto Rican rum	½ ounce curaçao
	4 ounces guava juice

Shake with 1 small scoop shaved ice. Pour into a 10-ounce glass.

Iced Rum and Coffee

1 ounce Barbados or Barbancourt 5-star rum	Cool strong coffee
1½ teaspoons bar sugar	Vanilla-flavored sweetened whipped cream
2 dashes fresh cream	

Pour rum, sugar, and cream over coffee in a tall glass. Fill glass with coffee. Top with a spoonful of whipped cream.

Iere Daiquiri (Trinidad Hilton)

1¼ ounces Trinidad white rum	½ ounce lime juice
½ ounce grenadine	

Shake with ice cubes. Strain into a chilled champagne glass. Decorate with a lime slice.

Indian Summer Drink

Juice of ½ lemon
1 teaspoon bar sugar
1½ ounces light Puerto Rican
  rum

1 egg yolk
Club soda

Shake lemon juice, sugar, rum, and egg yolk well with ice cubes. Strain into a 10-ounce glass. Fill glass with soda.

Indies Coconut Daiquiri

1½ ounces dark Virgin Islands
  rum
2 ounces Lopez coconut cream

1 ounce lemon juice
½ ounce Simple Syrup (see
  Index)

Blend with ½ cup shaved ice in an electric drink mixer until thick. Pour into a chilled large saucer champagne glass.

Jamaica Daiquiri

2 ounces white Jamaica rum
½ ounce maraschino liqueur
¾ ounce fresh grapefruit juice

Juice of 1 lime
1 teaspoon rock candy syrup

Blend with a 10-ounce glass of shaved ice in an electric drink mixer (or in a shaker can with mixing glass). Pour into a large champagne glass.

Jamaica Delight

2 ounces Appleton Special or
  white Jamaica rum
½ ounce Triple Sec

3 ounces pineapple juice
¼ ounce lime juice

Pack a 10-ounce glass with shaved ice. Blend ingredients together in an electric drink mixer. Pour into the prepared glass. Decorate with a maraschino cherry and, if you wish, a slice of pineapple. Serve with a straw.

Jamaica Float

Juice of ½ lime   2 ounces club soda
1 dash rock candy syrup   1 ounce dark Jamaica rum

Stir lime juice, syrup, and sparkling water well with ice cubes in a sour glass. Decorate with a maraschino cherry. Float rum.

Jamaica Rum Sour

2 ounces golden Jamaica rum   3 dashes fresh lemon juice
1 ounce club soda   1 teaspon bar sugar

Shake with shaved ice. Strain into a chilled sour glass. Garnish with a half slice of orange and a maraschino cherry. VARIATION: Substitute another rum of your choice for golden Jamaica rum.

Jamaica Rumhattan

1½ ounces light Jamaica rum
1½ ounces dry vermouth

Pour over ice cubes in an old-fashioned glass. Stir well.

Jamaica Sec

1½ ounces light or medium Jamaica rum
1 dash Angostura bitters

Pour over ice cubes in an old-fashioned glass. Stir.

Jamestown Sour

2 ounces golden Puerto Rican   1 ounce orange juice
   rum   ½ ounce lemon juice
1 teaspoon bar sugar

Shake well with shaved ice. Strain into a chilled sour glass. Decorate with an orange slice and a maraschino cherry.

Kona Gold

Juice of 1 lime, hand-squeezed
1 teaspoon bar sugar
1 dash maraschino liqueur

1 ounce Lemon Hart Golden
Jamaica rum
2 dashes Herbsaint

Blend lime juice, sugar, maraschino, and rum with 1 scoop shaved ice in an electric drink mixer. Strain through a medium-mesh kitchen strainer into a tiki stem champagne glass or 4½-ounce champagne glass. Float Herbsaint.

La Florida Daiquiri

This is a drink that must be made correctly. Try this experiment to prove what I say: Cut a lime in half and squeeze the juice by hand into the mixing container until there is no more juice left in the lime, then go on making the drink. Now, with another container, squeeze the juice in a lemon squeezer. Taste them both and see how much more bitter the second will be—because of the oils in the peel that were squeezed by the lemon squeezer. The difference is unbelievable.

2 ounces light Puerto Rican rum
1 teaspoon maraschino liqueur

1 teaspoon bar sugar
Juice of 1 lime, hand-squeezed

Blend with a scant ½ scoop of shaved ice in an electric drink mixer. Pour, frappéed, into a chilled champagne glass.

La Florida Rum Daisy

If you have chartreuse on hand, you can make this nice drink. If you haven't got any, make something else. It won't work with anything but chartreuse.

½ teaspoon bar sugar
1 dash Angostura bitters

½ teaspoon yellow chartreuse
2 ounces light Puerto Rican rum

Put into an old-fashioned glass filled with ice cubes. Stir. Decorate with the spiral-cut peel of ½ lemon, several mint sprigs, 2 maraschino cherries, and sliced fruits in season.

Leilani Grass Hut

2 ounces light Puerto Rican or
   Hawaiian rum
1 dash grenadine
½ ounce lemon juice

½ ounce pineapple juice
½ ounce papaya juice
1 ounce orange juice
Club soda

Pour all ingredients except soda into a tall highball glass nearly filled with ice cubes. Stir well. Fill glass with soda. Add a maraschino cherry and a pineapple slice.

Leilani Volcano

4 ounces light Puerto Rican or
   Hawaiian rum
2 ounces pineapple juice

1 ounce papaya juice
1 teaspoon bar sugar
Juice of 1 lime

Shake with ice cubes. Pour over ice cubes in a highball glass. Garnish with fresh fruit.

Lichee Nut Daiquiri

1½ ounces light Puerto Rican
   rum
1 dash maraschino liqueur

Juice of 1 lime
1 dash rock candy syrup
3 whole canned lichee nuts

Blend with a 12-ounce glass of shaved ice in an electric drink mixer. Pour into a tiki stem champagne glass or other large saucer champagne glass.

Mahukona

1 ounce light Puerto Rican rum
½ ounce Triple Sec
2 dashes Angostura bitters

1 dash rock candy syrup
½ ounce lemon juice
½ slice pineapple

Blend with ½ scoop shaved ice in an electric drink mixer. Pour into a 10-ounce pilsner glass half filled with shaved ice. Decorate with fresh mint and a fruit stick.

Mai Tai

One of the finest drinks I ever concocted was made with seventeen-year-old Jamaican rum. I was behind my bar one day in 1944 talking with my bartender, and I told him that I was going to make the finest rum drink in the world. Just then Ham and Carrie Guild, some old friends from Tahiti, came in. I told them I was concocting the world's finest rum drink and asked them to try it. Carrie tasted it, raised her glass, and said, "Mai Tai—Roa Ae," which in Tahitian means "Out of this world—the best!" That's the name of the drink, I said, and we named it Mai Tai.

Within two years, we had used up all of the seventeen-year-old Jamaica rum in the world because of the popularity of the Mai Tai; and there was no more. As a substitute, I blended my own Mai Tai rum. You can use it to make Mai Tais today.

Here is my original formula for the Mai Tai, as well as two contemporary formulas.

Mai Tai (Trader Vic's original)

2 ounces seventeen-year-old J. Wray and Nephew Jamaica rum
½ ounce Holland deKuyper orange curaçao
½ ounce French Garnier orgeat
¼ ounce rock candy syrup
Juice of 1 lime

Hand-shake and then garnish with half of the lime shell inside the drink and float a sprig of fresh mint at the edge of the drink. The drink should be chilled nicely with a considerable amount of shaved ice in a 15-ounce glass.

Mai Tai

1 lime
2 ounces Trader Vic Mai Tai rum
½ ounce orange curaçao
¼ ounce rock candy syrup
¼ ounce orgeat syrup

Cut lime in half; squeeze juice over shaved ice in a Mai Tai (double old-fashioned) glass; save 1 spent shell. Add remaining ingredients and enough shaved ice to fill glass. Hand-shake. Decorate with the spent lime shell, fresh mint, and a fruit stick.

Mai Tai (using commercial mix)

2 ounces Trader Vic Mai Tai mix
2 ounces Trader Vic Mai Tai rum

Fill a Mai Tai (double old-fashioned) glass with shaved ice. Add mix and rum, and shake. Decorate with fresh mint and a fruit stick and fresh lime if you wish.

Mai Tai Rum Old-fashioned

1½ ounces Trader Vic Mai Tai   **½ ounce water**
  rum   **2 dashes maraschino cherry juice**
2 dashes Peychaud bitters

Pour into a 10-ounce old-fashioned glass filled with ice cubes. Stir well. Add a twist of lemon peel. Decorate with a fruit stick and fresh mint.

Mango Daiquiri

1 ounce light Puerto Rican rum   **1 piece mango**
1 dash maraschino liqueur   **1 dash rock candy syrup**
1 lime

Blend thoroughly with 1 scoop shaved ice in an electric drink mixer. Pour into a large tiki stem champagne glass or other 4½-ounce champagne glass.

Menehune Juice

You can't see or talk to a menehune until you drink some Menehune Juice. So drink some.

1 lime   **½ ounce orange curaçao**
2 ounces Trader Vic light Puerto   **¼ ounce rock candy syrup**
  Rican rum   **¼ ounce orgeat syrup**

Squeeze lime juice over shaved ice in a Mai Tai (double old-fashioned) glass; save 1 shell. Add remaining ingredients and enough shaved ice to fill glass. Hand-shake. Decorate with the spent lime shell, fresh mint, and a menehune.

Menehune Juice (using commercial mix)

2 ounces Trader Vic Mai Tai mix
2 ounces Trader Vic light Puerto Rican rum

Fill a Mai Tai (double old-fashioned) glass with shaved ice. Add mix and rum, and shake. Decorate with fresh mint and a menehune and fresh lime if you wish.

Miami Mule

If you don't have Siegert's Bouquet rum, use light Puerto Rican rum instead.

1 lime   **Ginger beer**
2 ounces Siegert's Bouquet rum

Squeeze lime juice into mug; add lime shells. Pack mug with shaved ice. Pour in rum. Fill with ginger beer. Stir gently.

Mr. Nephew's Daiquiri

This is a great drink. Very expensive.

1 ounce J. Wray and Nephew   **Juice of 1 lime**
fifteen-year special reserve rum   **1 teaspoon bar sugar**
1 dash maraschino liqueur

Blend in an electric drink mixer with 1 scoop shaved ice. Strain through a medium-mesh kitchen strainer into a chilled tiki stem or other large saucer champagne glass.

Molokai Mike

1 ounce light Puerto Rican rum   **½ ounce orgeat syrup**
½ ounce brandy   **½ ounce Rhum Negrita**
1 ounce orange juice   **1 dash grenadine**
1 ounce lemon juice

Blend with 1 small scoop shaved ice the first 5 ingredients in an electric drink mixer. Pour into bottom half of a Molokai Mike glass or footed vase-shaped glass. Blend with ½ scoop shaved ice the Rhum

Negrita and grenadine in an electric drink mixer. Slowly pour into top half of glass.

Native Boutique

2 ounces Barbancourt 5-star rum	**1 dash Angostura bitters**
1 egg	**1 dash Simple Syrup (see Index)**

Shake well in an electric drink mixer with ice cubes. Strain into a large chilled champagne glass. Decorate with a lime slice.

Navy Grog

You can substitute 3 ounces of Trader Vic Navy Grog and Punch rum for the 3 rums listed below.

1 ounce light Puerto Rican rum	**3 ounces Trader Vic Navy Grog**
1 ounce dark Jamaica rum	**mix**
1 ounce 86-proof Demerara	
rum	

Pour into a Mai Tai (double old-fashioned) glass filled with shaved ice. Hand-shake. Decorate with a rock candy stick, fresh mint, and fresh lime if you wish.

New Moon

½ lime	**½ ounce peach liqueur**
½ ounce dark Jamaica rum	**¼ ounce grenadine (scant**
1 ounce vodka	**measure)**
½ ounce Amer Picon	

Squeeze lime juice into a mixing glass with cracked ice; save shell. Add remaining ingredients. Shake. Pour into a 10-ounce pilsner glass. Add the spent lime shell.

Northside Special

2 ounces dark Jamaica rum	**2 teaspoons bar sugar**
Juice of 1 orange	**Club soda**
½ ounce lemon juice	

Stir together all ingredients except soda in a 12-ounce chimney glass with ice cubes. Fill glass with soda. Stir gently. Serve with straws.

Old Yellowstain

1½ ounces golden Puerto Rican rum
¾ ounce passion fruit nectar

1½ ounces Trader Vic Navy Grog mix

Shake with ice cubes. Pour into a footed iced tea glass. Decorate with a rock candy stick and fresh mint.

Orange Rum Shrub

1 pound bar sugar
1 quart orange juice

2 quarts rum of your choice

Stir sugar with orange juice until dissolved. Add rum and mix well. Cover and let stand for 3 or 4 weeks. Strain and bottle. If you wish to add the flavor of orange peel, add a few orange peelings to the rum for 12 hours. To serve, pour over shaved ice in tall glasses. Makes about 15 servings.

Outrigger Tiara

1 ounce light Puerto Rican rum
1 ounce dark Jamaica rum
1 dash grenadine

1 dash curaçao
1 ounce orange juice
1 ounce lemon juice

Blend with 1 scoop shaved ice in an electric drink mixer. Pour into an individual scorpion bowl or wide-bowled individual compote. Add ice cubes. Decorate with a gardenia.

P.B.2Y2

During World War II we had a lot of Navy fliers who flew P.B.2Y2 planes to Alaska and the South Pacific. Whenever they could, those fliers would get some booze from me to take away for their pals who needed a drink. It became quite a project, fun, and not frowned upon at all—not even by CO's. We were able to distribute hundreds

and hundreds of bottles of cheer during that time. We later made this
drink in honor of those fliers in those times.

1½ ounces light Puerto Rican rum	½ ounce curaçao
1 ounce dark Jamaica rum	Juice of ½ lime
¼ ounce grenadine	1½ ounces orange juice
	¾ ounce lemon juice

Blend with ½ scoop shaved ice in an electric drink mixer. Pour into
an individual scorpion bowl or wide-bowled individual compote. Decorate with a gardenia.

Piña Colada

2 ounces golden Puerto Rican rum
3 ounces unsweetened pineapple juice

Blend in an electric drink mixer with 1 scoop of shaved ice for 10
to 20 seconds. Pour over ice cubes in a tall 10-ounce glass. Serve with
a straw. VARIATION: Add 1 pineapple slice.

Pink Harmony

2 ounces Barbancourt 5-star rum	¼ ounce grenadine
¼ ounce maraschino liqueur	½ ounce lemon juice

Shake with ice cubes. Strain into a chilled champagne glass.

Pink Planet

3 ounces Barbancourt 5-star rum	½ ounce grenadine
2 ounces white Dubonnet	2 teaspoons lime or lemon juice

Blend with ½ cup shaved ice in an electric drink mixer. Pour into
2 chilled champagne glasses.

Pino Frío

1 ounce light Puerto Rican rum	2 slices pineapple
2 ounces unsweetened pineapple juice	¼ ounce lemon juice
	1 dash rock candy syrup

Blend thoroughly with 1 scoop shaved ice in an electric drink mixer. Pour into a planter's punch glass or 12½-ounce tumbler.

Pino Pepe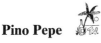

1 ounce light Puerto Rican rum
½ ounce Triple Sec
1 ounce vodka
Juice of ½ lime

¼ ounce lemon juice
2 ounces unsweetened pineapple
   juice
1 dash rock candy syrup

Blend with 1 scoop shaved ice in an electric drink mixer. Pour into hollowed-out fresh baby pineapple or ceramic pineapple. Add ice cubes. Serve with straws.

Ponce de León

½ ounce golden Puerto Rican
   rum
½ ounce brandy

½ ounce Cointreau
½ ounce grapefruit juice
Champagne

Shake rum, brandy, Cointreau, and grapefruit juice with ice cubes. Strain into a chilled champagne glass. Fill glass with champagne.

Potted Parrot

2 ounces light Puerto Rican rum
½ ounce curaçao
¼ ounce rock candy syrup

¼ ounce orgeat syrup
1 ounce lemon juice
2 ounces orange juice

Shake well with ½ scoop shaved ice. Pour into a ten-pin pilsner glass. Decorate with a mint sprig. Serve with straws.

Pussyfoot

3 ounces white Jamaica rum
2 ounces fresh cream
2½ ounces pineapple juice

2½ ounces lime juice
2 ounces maraschino cherry
   juice

Blend in an electric drink blender with 1 scoop ice for 15 seconds. Pour into 2 chimney glasses. Fill with ice cubes. Garnish each drink with a maraschino cherry and an orange half slice.

Rainbow Grog

2 cans (12 ounces each) V-8 juice
¼ teaspoon ground ginger

1 ounce tomato catsup
8 or 9 ounces light Puerto Rican rum

Heat V-8 juice, ginger, and catsup together in a saucepan. Remove from heat. Stir in rum. Pour into 6 bouillon cups. Garnish each with a lemon half slice.

Rhum Cosmo

Louis Gardère of the Haitian Barbancourt rum family and, incidentally, a delegate to the United Nations Charter signing in San Francisco in 1945, tells of going to our Trader Vic bar in our restaurant in New York in the Plaza Hotel. Knowing that Barbancourt 5-star rum is a required ingredient for this Rhum Cosmo drink, he ordered it. But he also ordered the same drink made the exact same way except with 3-star Barbancourt (a slightly lesser rum) rather than 5-star. He wanted to taste them, side by side, to check his own hunch that, in a mixed drink, the slight difference in rum quality would not show. He thought the 3-star drink would taste just as good as the 5-star. But when he tried them both, there was all the difference in the world. And he had to admit that Trader Vic knows his rum flavors. I am not trying to blow smoke up my own chimney by telling this. I am trying to point out that you can't make a silk purse out of a sow's ear.

This drink is named after Cosmo Alley, where our San Francisco restaurant is located.

1½ ounces Barbancourt 5-star rum
Juice of ½ lime

1 dash rock candy syrup
1 ounce unsweetened pineapple juice

Shake with 1 scoop shaved ice. Pour into footed iced tea glass. Decorate with a long spear of fresh pineapple and fresh mint.

Rock and Rum

1½ ounces light Puerto Rican rum
Quinine water

Pour rum over ice cubes in an old-fashioned glass. Add a splash of quinine water. Twist lemon peel over drink.

Roman Candle

3 ounces Barbados rum   Juice of ½ lime
1 teaspoon bar sugar   Tom collins mix or Squirt

Stir rum, sugar, and lime juice with ice cubes in a 12-ounce chimney glass filled with ice cubes. Fill glass with tom collins mix or Squirt. Dust with ground cinnamon.

Royal Daiquiri (Don the Beachcomber)

1½ ounces light Puerto Rican   ½ ounce parfait amour
   rum   ¼ teaspoon bar sugar
½ ounce lime juice

Blend with ½ scoop shaved ice in an electric drink mixer for 10 to 20 seconds. Pour into a 6-ounce champagne glass.

Rum and Coffee Whipped Cream

1 large scoop vanilla, coffee, or   Chilled black coffee
   chocolate ice cream   Whipped cream
1½ ounces Barbancourt 5-star
   rum

Put ice cream into a tall glass. Add rum. Fill glass with coffee. Top with a spoonful of whipped cream.

Rum and Ginger

1½ ounces rum of your choice
Ginger ale

Place 2 or 3 ice cubes in an 8-ounce highball glass. Add rum. Fill glass with ginger ale. Stir gently.

Rum and Iced Tea

1 ounce light Puerto Rican rum   Cool freshly brewed tea
Juice of ⅛ lime or lemon   Bar sugar to taste

Pour rum and lime or lemon juice over ice cubes in a tall glass. Fill glass with tea. Add sugar to taste. Decorate with a mint sprig.

Rum and Maple

1 teaspoon maple syrup   1½ ounces light Puerto Rican
1 dash Angostura bitters   rum

Muddle maple syrup and bitters with a splash of water in an old-fashioned glass. Add 1 ice cube and the rum. Stir. Add a twist of lemon peel.

Rum and Soda

1½ ounces rum of your choice
Club soda

Place 2 or 3 ice cubes in an 8-ounce highball glass. Add rum. Fill glass with soda. Stir gently.

Rum and Tonic

2 ounces light Puerto Rican rum   Quinine water
2 thin lemon slices

Pour rum into a highball glass filled with ice cubes. Add lemon. Fill glass with quinine water. Stir lightly.

Rum Boogie

2 ounces Trader Vic rum and   1 dash Herbsaint
   brandy (or half light Puerto   3 ounces orange juice
   Rican rum and half brandy)   2 ounces lemon juice
1 ounce 151-proof Demerara rum   1 ounce pineapple juice
1 dash curaçao   1 dash rock candy syrup

Blend with 1 scoop shaved ice in an electric drink mixer. Pour into a tiki bowl. Decorate with a gardenia.

Rum Cobbler

3 ounces Barbancourt 5-star rum   1 teaspoon bar sugar
1 ounce pineapple juice or
   apricot nectar (juice)

Pack a 10-ounce glass with shaved ice. Shake ingredients together in an electric drink mixer and pour into the prepared glass. Churn vigorously with a long barspoon to create a frost on the glass. Decorate with a fruit stick or a fresh mint sprig.

Rum Collins

1 ounce lemon juice
½ ounce Simple Syrup (see
  Index)

1 ounce light Puerto Rican rum
½ lime
Club soda

Pour lemon juice, syrup, and rum into a 12-ounce chimney glass filled with ice cubes. Squeeze in lime juice; save shell. Fill with soda. Stir well. Decorate with the spent lime shell and a fruit stick. Serve with straws. VARIATION: Use half light Puerto Rican rum and half dark Jamaican rum.

Rum Daisy—1

½ lime
1½ ounces light Puerto Rican
  rum

1 dash grenadine

Squeeze lime juice into a shaker over 1 scoop shaved ice; save lime shell. Add rum and grenadine. Shake. Pour, unstrained, into an old-fashioned glass. Add the spent lime shell.

Rum Daisy—2

Juice of ½ lemon
2 dashes grenadine

1 ounce Siegert's Bouquet rum
Club soda

Pour lemon juice, grenadine, and rum into a highball glass or goblet filled with shaved ice. Fill with soda. Stir gently. Decorate with fresh fruit.

Rum Flip

1 ounce Barbancourt 5-star rum
1 ounce sweet sherry
1 egg

1 ounce heavy cream
1 teaspoon bar sugar

Shake well with ice cubes. Strain into a chilled fizz glass.

Rum Float

Juice of ½ lime
1 teaspoon bar sugar
3 ounces club soda

1 ounce Jamaica or Puerto Rican
  rum

Stir lime juice and sugar with ice cubes in a 6-ounce glass. Add soda and stir lightly. Float rum on top.

Rum, Gum, and Lime

½ lime
1 dash rock candy syrup

1 ounce light Puerto Rican
  rum

Squeeze lime juice over ice cubes in an old-fashioned glass. Drop in the shell. Add syrup and rum. Stir. Decorate with a fruit stick.

Rum Hawaii

1½ ounces light Puerto Rican
  rum
1 ounce pineapple juice

1 dash orange bitters
1 egg white

Shake with ice cubes. Strain into a chilled 4-ounce wine glass.

Rum Jumbie

1½ ounces light Virgin Islands or
  Puerto Rican rum
½ ounce grenadine

½ ounce lime juice
2 ounces pineapple juice
2 ounces orange juice

Stir together well with ice cubes in a tall glass.

Rum Keg

5 ounces light Puerto Rican
  rum
1 ounce dark Jamaica rum
1 ounce rock candy syrup

1 ounce passion fruit nectar
2 ounces pineapple juice
4 ounces lemon juice
1 ounce apricot liqueur

Blend with 2 scoops shaved ice in an electric drink mixer. Pour into a ceramic rum keg. Add ice cubes. Makes 4 servings.

Rum Mist

1½ ounces light Puerto Rican rum
1 dash Angostura bitters

Pour rum into an old-fashioned glass packed with shaved ice. Add bitters and a twist of lemon peel. VARIATION: Substitute Barbancourt 5-star rum for the light Puerto Rican rum and omit bitters.

Rum Mocha

2 ounces light Puerto Rican   **2 scoops vanilla ice cream**
  rum   **Cool strong black coffee**

Fill a 14-ounce glass halfway with shaved ice. Add rum and ice cream. Fill glass with coffee. Stir.

Rum on the Rocks

Pour 1½ ounces of your favorite rum over ice cubes in an old-fashioned glass. Add a twist of lemon peel. Stir.

Rum Pick-me-up

1 ounce Barbancourt 5-star rum   **Chilled champagne**
1 teaspoon bar sugar

Shake rum and sugar with ice cubes. Strain into a chilled champagne glass. Fill glass with champagne.

Rum Pickup (Caneel Bay Plantation)

2 ounces dark Virgin Islands rum   **Club soda**
2 ounces milk

Pour rum and milk into a 10-ounce glass filled with ice cubes. Stir. Fill with chilled soda. Stir gently.

Rum Pot

3 ounces Trader Vic Navy Grog and Punch rum
3 ounces lemon juice
3 ounces orange juice

3 dashes vanilla extract
¾ ounce passion fruit nectar
1 ounce rock candy syrup

Blend with 2 scoops shaved ice in an electric drink mixer. Pour into 2 sugar pots or a large bowl over cracked ice. Makes 2 drinks.

Rum Ramsey

This was originated by Albert Martin in the Bon Ton Bar on Magazine Street in New Orleans. He used to turn his back and make the drinks on the back of the bar so no one could see him. Finally, I told him that I'd come to New Orleans just so I could learn how to make drinks. And then he taught me all he knew—because I was interested. Sweet guy, Albert Martin.

1½ ounces light Puerto Rican rum
1 teaspoon Bourbon

½ teaspoon bar sugar
1 dash Peychaud bitters
Juice of ¼ lime

Stir with ice cubes. Strain into a chilled cocktail glass.

Rum Rickey

Juice of ½ lime
2 ounces light Puerto Rican rum
½ teaspoon Simple Syrup (see Index), orgeat, or Falernum

Club soda

Pour lime juice, rum, and syrup over 2 ice cubes in an 8-ounce glass. Stir well. Fill glass with chilled soda. Stir gently.

Rum Sazerac

1 dash Peychaud bitters
1 dash Simple Syrup (see Index)

2 ounces light Puerto Rican rum
Pernod

Stir bitters, syrup, and rum well with ice cubes in an old-fashioned glass. Strain into an old-fashioned glass that has been coated inside with Pernod. Add a twist of lemon peel.

Rum Screwdriver

1½ ounces Barbados rum
3 ounces orange juice

Pour over ice cubes in an old-fashioned glass. Stir.

Rum Sour

1½ ounces Barbados rum   **1 teaspoon Simple Syrup (see**
Juice of ½ lemon   **Index)**

Shake well with ice cubes. Strain into a chilled sour glass. Decorate
with an orange slice and a maraschino cherry.

Rum Sour on the Rocks

1½ ounces light or golden rum   **1 teaspoon Simple Syrup (see**
Juice of ½ lemon   **Index)**

Shake well with ice cubes. Strain into an old-fashioned glass filled
with ice cubes. Decorate with an orange slice and a maraschino
cherry.

Rum Toddy (cold)

½ teaspoon bar sugar   **2 ounces light Puerto Rican rum**
2 teaspoons water

Stir sugar and water in an old-fashioned glass. Add rum and 1 ice
cube. Stir. Add a twist of lemon peel.

Samoan Fog Cutter

1½ ounces light Puerto Rican   **½ ounce orgeat syrup**
** rum**   **2 ounces lemon juice**
½ ounce brandy   **1 ounce orange juice**
½ ounce gin   **¼ ounce sweet sherry**

Blend all ingredients except sherry in an electric drink mixer with
1 scoop shaved ice. Pour into Fog Cutter mug or other large mug.
Add ice cubes. Float sherry. Decorate with fresh mint and a stirrer.

Samson's Dilly

1 ounce 86-proof Demerara rum   **1 dash rock candy syrup**
1 dash Peychaud bitters   **½ ounce plain water**

Stir with ice cubes in an old-fashioned glass. Add a twist of lemon peel. Decorate with a fruit stick.

San Juan Frappé

1 ounce light Puerto Rican rum   **1 tablespoon Lopez coconut**
½ ounce grapefruit juice   **cream or powdered coconut**

Shake with 1 scoop shaved ice in an electric drink mixer. Pour into a chilled champagne glass.

Scorpion (individual)

2 ounces light Puerto Rican rum   **2 ounces orange juice**
1 ounce brandy   **½ ounce orgeat syrup**
1½ ounces lemon juice

Blend with 1 scoop shaved ice in an electric drink mixer. Pour into a scorpion bowl or wide-bowled individual compote. Add ice cubes. Decorate with a gardenia.

Scorpion (for 3 or 4 people)

6 ounces light Puerto Rican rum   **4 ounces lemon juice**
1 ounce brandy   **1½ ounces orgeat syrup**
6 ounces orange juice

Blend with 2 scoops shaved ice in an electric drink mixer. Pour into a large scorpion bowl or large compote. Fill with ice cubes. Decorate with a gardenia. Serve with 3 or 4 straws.

Señor Bailey

6 sprigs fresh mint   **¼ ounce lime juice**
1 teaspoon bar sugar   **2 ounces light Puerto Rican rum**

In a tall goblet, muddle mint with sugar and lime juice. Fill glass with shaved ice and add rum. Stir until glass frosts. Garnish with additional mint. Serve with straws.

Shady Lady

3 ounces Barbancourt 5-star rum	½ tablespoon lemon juice
1 dash Grand Marnier	1 tablespoon heavy fresh cream
1 teaspoon bar sugar	1 egg white

Shake with ½ cup shaved ice in an electric drink mixer. Pour into 2 chilled 8-ounce glasses.

Shark's Tooth—1

½ lime	½ ounce lemon juice
1 ounce Ronrico 151-proof rum	1 dash rock candy syrup
1 dash grenadine	2 ounces club soda

Squeeze lime juice over ice cubes in a 10-ounce pilsner glass; save shell. Add remaining ingredients. Stir well. Decorate with the spent lime shell, fresh mint, and a fruit stick.

Shark's Tooth—2

1½ ounces Trader Vic Navy Grog and Punch rum	¼ ounce lemon juice
¼ ounce dry vermouth	1 dash passion fruit nectar
¼ ounce sloe gin	Club soda

Stir all ingredients except soda with ice cubes. Strain into a 10-ounce glass filled with shaved ice. Fill glass with soda. Serve with straws.

Shark's Tooth—3

2½ ounces light Puerto Rican rum	1 ounce lemon juice
½ ounce grenadine	Club soda

Stir rum, lemon juice, and grenadine with ice cubes. Strain into a 10-ounce glass filled with shaved ice. Fill glass with soda. Serve with straws.

Shingle Stain

2 ounces Trader Vic Mai Tai
  rum
2 dashes Angostura bitters
¼ ounce grenadine

1½ ounces cranberry juice
½ ounce pineapple juice
Juice of 1 lime

Shake with ice cubes. Pour into a ten-pin pilsner glass. Decorate with fresh mint.

Siboney

1 ounce dark Jamaica rum
½ ounce lemon juice
½ ounce unsweetened pineapple
  juice

½ ounce passion fruit nectar

Shake and strain into a chilled tiki stem champagne glass or other large saucer champagne glass.

Sly Mongoose

2 ounces dark Jamaica rum
2 ounces pineapple juice

2 ounces orange juice

Pour into a 10-ounce glass filled with shaved ice. Stir.

Space Needle

1½ ounces light Puerto Rican
  rum
1½ ounces dark Jamaica rum

1 ounce curaçao
1½ ounces lemon juice.
¾ ounce orgeat syrup

Blend with 1 scoop shaved ice in an electric drink mixer. Pour into a 10-ounce glass. Add shaved ice to fill glass. Serve with a straw.

Suffering Bastard

1 ounce light Puerto Rican rum
2 ounces Rhum St. James

3 ounces Trader Vic Mai Tai
  mix

Pour rums and mix into a Mai Tai (double old-fashioned) glass filled with shaved ice. Hand-shake. Decorate with a lengthwise strip of cucumber peel, fresh mint, a fruit stick, and lime if you wish.

Sun and Shadow

2½ ounces dark Jamaica rum
¾ ounce 151-proof light rum
½ ounce apricot brandy

2 ounces pineapple juice
Juice of ½ lime

Shake with ice cubes. Pour into a 14-ounce glass. Add ice cubes to fill glass.

Surf-rider

2 ounces light Puerto Rican rum
2 ounces cranberry juice

2 ounces apple juice
1 dash lemon juice

Pour over ice cubes in a highball glass. Stir to blend. Garnish with a sprig of mint.

Swashbuckler (Buccaneer Hotel, St. Croix)

1½ ounces light Virgin Islands
   rum
Juice of 1 lime

1 teaspoon bar sugar
1 split champagne

Stir rum, lime juice, and sugar with shaved ice in a tall glass. Slowly add champagne.

Tabu

1 ounce light Puerto Rican rum
1 ounce vodka
1½ ounces unsweetened
   pineapple juice

½ ounce lemon juice
1 dash rock candy syrup

Blend with 1 scoop shaved ice in an electric drink mixer. Pour into a ceramic coconut. Decorate with fresh mint and a fruit stick.

Tahitian Gold

Juice of 1 lime	1 ounce Rhum St. James
1 teaspoon bar sugar	1 dash Herbsaint
1 dash maraschino liqueur	

Blend lime juice, sugar, maraschino, and rum with 1 scoop shaved ice in an electric drink mixer. Strain through a medium-mesh kitchen strainer into a tiki stem champagne glass or other large saucer champagne glass. Top with Herbsaint.

Tahitian Pearl

1 ounce light Puerto Rican rum	1 dash rock candy syrup
¼ ounce maraschino liqueur	Juice of 1 lime

Shake with ice cubes. Pour, with small ice cubes, into a tiki stem champagne compote or 10-ounce champagne compote. Decorate with a pearl on a gardenia petal.

Test Pilot

¾ ounce light Puerto Rican rum	¼ ounce Cointreau
1¾ ounces dark Jamaica rum	¼ ounce lemon juice
¼ ounce Falernum	

Shake with ice cubes. Pour into a 10-ounce glass.

Tiara Tahiti

3 ounces light Puerto Rican rum	3 ounces orange juice
½ ounce brandy	3 ounces lemon juice
1½ ounces orgeat syrup	

Blend with 1½ scoops shaved ice in an electric drink mixer. Pour into a large scorpion bowl or large compote. Add ice cubes. Decorate with a gardenia. Makes 2 servings.

Tiki Bowl

1 ounce light Puerto Rican rum	2 ounces orange juice
1 ounce dark Jamaica rum	1½ ounces lemon juice
1 ounce brandy	½ ounce orgeat syrup

Blend with 1 scoop shaved ice in an electric drink mixer. Pour into a tiki bowl. Add ice cubes. Decorate with a gardenia.

Tiki Puka Puka

1 ounce light Puerto Rican rum
1 ounce dark Jamaica rum
1 ounce 151-proof Demerara
  rum
1 ounce orange juice

3 ounces Trader Vic Navy Grog
  mix
1 dash grenadine
Orange flower water

Blend with 1 scoop shaved ice all ingredients except orange flower water in an electric drink mixer. Pour into a grapefruit supreme glass or wide-bowled individual compote. Add ice cubes. Decorate with a gardenia. Dash orange flower water on gardenia.

Torch

2 ounces white Jamaica rum
¾ ounce passion fruit nectar
¾ ounce pineapple juice

1 ounce cranberry juice
Juice of ½ lime

Shake with ice cubes. Pour into a ten-pin pilsner glass.

Tortuga

½ lime
1 ounce lemon juice
1½ ounces orange juice
1 dash grenadine
1 dash crème de cacao

1 dash curaçao
1 ounce sweet vermouth
1¼ ounces 151-proof Demerara
  rum

Squeeze lime juice over ½ scoop shaved ice in container of an electric drink mixer; save shell. Add remaining ingredients. Blend. Pour into a 14-ounce tall footed highball glass. Add ice cubes. Decorate with the spent lime shell, fresh mint, and a stirrer.

Trader Vic Daiquiri

1 lime
1 teaspoon bar sugar
½ ounce Garnier maraschino
2 ounces light Puerto Rican rum

¼ teaspoon unsweetened frozen
  Florida grapefruit juice
  concentrate, undiluted

Finger-squeeze lime juice over a 12-ounce glass of shaved ice in container of an electric drink mixer. Add remaining ingredients. Blend. Strain through a medium-mesh kitchen strainer into a chilled tiki stem champagne glass or other large saucer champagne glass.

Trader Vic Flip

2 ounces Trader Vic Rum and
 Brandy (or half light Puerto
 Rican rum and half brandy)

1 teaspoon bar sugar
1 egg

Shake well with ice cubes. Strain into an 8-ounce fizz glass. Dust with ground cinnamon.

Trader Vic Grog

2 ounces dark Jamaica rum
1 dash Angostura bitters
1 ounce lemon juice

1 ounce passion fruit nectar
1 ounce unsweetened pineapple
 juice

Pour into a mixing glass filled with shaved ice. Shake. Pour into a ten-pin pilsner glass. Decorate with fresh mint, a maraschino cherry, and a stirrer.

Trader Vic Rum Bloody Mary

Same as bloody mary *except* substitute light Puerto Rican rum for vodka.

Tropical Itch

½ ounce light Virgin Islands or
 Puerto Rican rum
2 ounces vodka

¼ ounce Grand Marnier
6 ounces mango juice

Shake with 1 scoop shaved ice. Pour into a double old-fashioned glass.

Voodoo Grog

1 ounce golden Puerto Rican rum
2 ounces Rhum St. James
2 ounces Trader Vic Navy Grog
 mix

2 barspoons honey
½ ounce passion fruit nectar
1 egg white

Blend with 1 scoop shaved ice in an electric drink mixer. Pour into a Voodoo tumbler or other large tumbler. Add ice cubes. Dust with grated nutmeg. Decorate with fresh mint and a fruit stick.

Wahine

1 ounce light Puerto Rican rum
1 ounce vodka
½ ounce lemon juice

1½ ounces unsweetened
   pineapple juice
1 dash rock candy syrup

Blend with 1 scoop shaved ice in an electric drink mixer. Pour into a ceramic coconut. Add ice cubes. Decorate with fresh mint and a fruit stick.

Whaler's Toddy (cold)

2 ounces dark Jamaica rum
½ teaspoon brown sugar

Splash of water

Stir well with ice in an old-fashioned glass.

White Witch

½ lime
½ ounce white crème de cacao
½ ounce Cointreau

1 ounce white Jamaica rum
Club soda

Squeeze lime juice into a sling glass or 12-ounce tumbler filled with ice cubes; save shell. Add to glass crème de cacao, Cointreau, and rum. Add soda to fill glass. Stir. Decorate with the spent lime shell and fresh mint dusted with bar sugar.

Zombie

1 ounce light Puerto Rican rum
1 ounce dark Jamaica rum
¼ ounce grenadine
1 ounce curaçao

Juice of ½ lime
1½ ounces orange juice
1 ounce lemon juice

Blend with 1 scoop shaved ice in an electric drink mixer. Pour into a 14-ounce block optic chimney glass. Decorate with fresh mint and a stirrer.

EGGNOGS AND MILK PUNCHES AND LITTLE GOODIES

Apricot Nog

4 ounces Barbancourt 5-star rum
1 ounce apricot brandy or
   curaçao

½ cup apricot nectar (juice)
½ cup heavy cream
1 egg

Blend with ½ scoop shaved ice in an electric drink mixer. Pour into 2 chilled 10-ounce glasses.

Baltimore Eggnog—1

1 ounce brandy
1½ ounces madeira wine
½ ounce Jamaica rum
2 teaspoons Simple Syrup (see
   Index)

1 egg
4 ounces milk

Shake vigorously with ice cubes. Strain into a 12-ounce glass. Add cold milk to fill glass. Stir gently. Dust with grated nutmeg.

Baltimore Eggnog—2

1 ounce Bourbon
1 ounce madeira wine
2 ounces milk

1 egg
1 teaspoon bar sugar

Shake with ice cubes. Strain into a tumbler. Dust with grated nutmeg.

Banana Cow

The Banana Cow is the greatest hangover drink as far as I'm concerned. People are in a rut serving bloody marys, and they really *kill* you rather than *cool* you. But milk is good for you, and bananas are good for your stomach. Many is a morning I could count a lot of people waiting for me to open my doors for·a Rum or Banana Cow to cool it, heal it, and cure it completely.

1 ounce Trader Vic light Puerto Rican rum	**1 teaspoon bar sugar**
1 dash Angostura bitters	**1 dash vanilla**
1 whole banana	**3 ounces milk**

Blend with ½ scoop shaved ice in an electric drink mixer. Serve in a planter's punch glass or 12½-ounce tumbler.

Boston Eggnog

A Boston Eggnog is not a true eggnog. But we've put it in, because maybe you'll like it.

If you don't want to shake it with ice cubes, whirl it all in an electric drink mixer with a little shaved ice.

1 egg yolk	**¼ ounce Jamaica rum**
¾ tablespoon bar sugar	**4 ounces madeira**
½ ounce brandy	**Chilled milk**

Beat egg yolk and sugar together. Add brandy, rum, madeira, and 1 cup milk. Shake with a 4-ounce glass of shaved ice. Strain into a large glass. Fill with cold milk. Stir gently. Dust with grated nutmeg.

Colonial American Eggnog

12 egg yolks	**1 fifth dark Puerto Rican rum**
2¼ cups bar sugar	**1 pint heavy cream, softly**
2 cups milk	**whipped**

Beat egg yolks until light colored. Gradually beat in sugar and beat until thick. Stir in milk and rum. Chill for 3 hours. Fold in whipped cream. Chill for 1 hour more. Sprinkle with grated nutmeg. Makes 20 servings.

Eggnog Punch

12 eggs, separated
1 pound bar sugar
3 quarts cold milk
4 ounces curaçao

3 ounces light Puerto Rican rum
3 ounces dark Jamaica rum
1 quart cognac

Beat egg whites until soft peaks form; gradually beat in 1 cup of the sugar and beat until stiff. Beat yolks with remaining sugar until thick and light. Gradually beat in very cold milk. Add curaçao, rums, and cognac, stirring very well; pour into punch bowl. Heap egg whites over top. Serve in punch cups or goblets. If desired, dust top of each with grated nutmeg. Makes 20 servings.

Holiday Eggnog

This is a good eggnog formula. However, if you want, add a little more brandy; and suit to your taste on the rum.

12 eggs, separated
2 cups bar sugar
1 teaspoon vanilla

1½ gallons cold milk
1 pint brandy
1 cup dark Jamaica rum

Beat egg yolks until thick; gradually add 1½ cups of the sugar and beat until thick and lemon-colored. Beat in vanilla and milk. Stir in brandy and rum, pouring them into milk mixture very slowly—almost as if adding oil to eggs when making mayonnaise. With clean beaters, beat whites until soft peaks form; gradually add remaining sugar and beat until whites are stiff. Spoon whites over the top of the milk mixture and sprinkle with nutmeg. At serving time, ladle off a hole in the topping, ladle liquid out of this opening, and break off a spoonful of the topping with each serving of eggnog. Makes 30 to 35 servings.

Hot Eggnog

1 egg yolk	1 ounce brandy
1 teaspoon bar sugar	Hot milk
1 ounce light rum	

Mix egg yolk and sugar in a heated mug. Add rum and brandy and stir thoroughly. Stirring constantly, fill mug with hot milk. Dust with grated nutmeg.

Hot Rum Milk Punch

1½ ounces golden Puerto Rican rum	1 dash Angostura bitters
1 teaspoon bar sugar	1 cup very hot milk

Blend in an electric drink mixer. Pour into a heated large mug. Dust with grated nutmeg.

Milk Punch

1 ounce Siegert's Bouquet rum	1 teaspoon bar sugar
½ pint milk	

Shake well in a commercial electric drink mixer (or in a shaker can with mixing glass) with ice cubes. Strain into a 10-ounce glass. Dust with grated nutmeg.

Milky Way

½ ounce light Jamaica rum	6 ounces milk
½ ounce brandy	3 drops vanilla
½ ounce Bourbon	

Shake well with 1 large scoop ice cubes in a commercial electric drink mixer (or in a shaker can with mixing glass). Pour into a 10-ounce glass. Add ice cubes to almost fill glass. Dust with grated nutmeg. Serve with a straw.

Rum Cow

This is a morning drink. It is especially good if you mix a little of any of the pungent rums with the Puerto Rican rum to make a fuller rum taste.

1 ounce light Puerto Rican rum   1 teaspoon bar sugar
1 dash Angostura bitters   6 ounces milk
1 dash vanilla

Shake in a commercial electric drink mixer (or in a shaker can with mixing glass) with ice cubes. Strain into a planter's punch glass or 12½-ounce tumbler. Dust with grated nutmeg.

Rum Eggnog

3 ounces dark Jamaica rum   1 dash vanilla
4 ounces milk   1 egg
2 teaspoons Simple Syrup (see
    Index)

Shake with ice cubes. Strain into a 10-ounce glass. Dust with grated nutmeg.

Rum Eggnog Punch

12 eggs, separated   Grated nutmeg
6 tablespoons bar sugar   1 bottle (fifth) Barbancourt 5-star
1 quart milk   or Barbados rum
1 pint heavy cream, whipped   ½ pint brandy

Beat egg whites until soft peaks form; gradually beat in 2 tablespoons of the sugar and beat until stiff. Beat egg yolks with the remaining 4 tablespoons sugar until thick and lemon-colored; gradually beat in milk and whipped cream. Add a few dashes of nutmeg. Gradually stir in rum and brandy. Fold in egg whites. Chill thoroughly. Makes 36 to 40 servings.

Rum Milk Punch

2 ounces light Puerto Rican rum   ½ pint milk
1 teaspoon bar sugar

Shake with ice cubes. Strain into a 12-ounce chimney glass. Dust with grated nutmeg.

Rum Puff

1 ounce Barbancourt 5-star rum   **Club soda**
1 ounce milk

Pour rum and milk over 3 cubes of ice in an 8-ounce highball glass. Stir. Fill glass with chilled soda. Stir gently.

Savannah

3 ounces Barbancourt 5-star rum   **½ cup heavy cream**
1 cup milk   **2 teaspoons bar sugar**

Blend with ½ cup shaved ice in an electric drink mixer. Pour into 2 chilled glasses.

Traditional American Eggnog

12 egg yolks   **1 bottle (fifth) golden rum**
½ pound bar sugar   **1 quart heavy cream, whipped**
1 quart milk

Beat egg yolks until light colored. Add sugar and beat until mixture is thick. Stir in milk and rum. Chill for 3 hours. Pour into a chilled punch bowl. Fold in cream. Chill for 1 hour more. Sprinkle with grated nutmeg. Makes 20 servings.

Fizzes, Slings & Sangarees

Maui Fizz

Same as Racquet Club Fizz (see Index).

Narragansett Fizz

2 ounces light Puerto Rican rum
1 tablespoon bar sugar
1 ounce lemon juice
2 ounces unsweetened pineapple
   juice

Club soda or lemon-lime
   carbonated beverage

Shake rum, sugar, lemon juice, and pineapple juice with shaved ice. Strain into a tall glass filled with ice cubes. Fill glass with chilled soda or lemon-lime beverage. Garnish with a lemon or lime slice.

New Orleans Rum Fizz

Juice of 1 lemon
Juice of ½ lime
1 egg white
3 barspoons bar sugar

1½ ounces light Puerto Rican
   rum
4 dashes orange flower water
1 ounce heavy cream

Pour all ingredients except cream into electric blender container; add ½ scoop shaved ice. Whirl, gradually adding cream; continue blending until liquefied. Pour into a 12-ounce chimney glass. Dust with grated nutmeg if you wish.

Pineapple Fizz

2 ounces pineapple juice
½ ounce lemon juice
1 teaspoon bar sugar

2 ounces light Puerto Rican rum
Carbonated water

Shake pineapple juice, lemon juice, sugar, and rum well with ice cubes. Strain into an 8-ounce highball glass. Fill glass with carbonated water. Stir gently.

Port-au-Prince Sling

2 ounces Barbancourt 5-star rum	**1 dash Angostura bitters**
¼ ounce kirsch	**1 dash club soda**
Juice of ½ lime	**1 teaspoon Benedictine**

Stir rum, kirsch, lime juice, and bitters with ice cubes in an old-fashioned glass. Add soda and stir gently. Float Benedictine.

Racquet Club Fizz

Here's a great drink for a festive morning party when you feel like going through the trouble. I call this my Racquet Club Fizz made in honor of a party at the Racquet Club in Honolulu in the late 1940s. Your guests will enjoy it.

1 ounce light Puerto Rican rum	**1 ounce lemon juice**
½ slice pineapple	**2 teaspoons bar sugar**
1 egg	

Blend with ½ scoop shaved ice in an electric drink mixer. Pour into a footed iced tea glass.

Rose of Haiti Fizz

1 ounce Barbancourt 5-star rum	**½ ounce grenadine**
½ ounce lime juice	**Club soda**

Shake rum, lime juice, and grenadine well with ice cubes. Strain into an 8-ounce highball glass filled with 3 ice cubes. Fill glass with chilled soda.

Rum Sangaree

3 ounces light Puerto Rican rum	**½ teaspoon lemon juice**
½ teaspoon Simple Syrup (see Index)	**Club soda**

Stir rum, syrup, and lemon juice well with ice cubes. Strain into an 8-ounce highball glass. Add 1 large ice cube. Fill glass with chilled soda or ice water. Dust with grated nutmeg.

Rum Silver Fizz

Silver fizzes have always been made with gin, but follow this recipe for a rum one. For a great variation, twist a slice of orange rind over it at the end.

1½ ounces Barbancourt 5-star or Barbados rum	1½ barspoons bar sugar
2 dashes Cointreau	1 egg white
½ ounce lime juice	¼ ounce cream
	Club soda

Blend all ingredients except soda in an electric drink mixer with 1 small scoop shaved ice. Pour into a highball glass. Fill glass with chilled soda.

San Juan Sling

1 part light Puerto Rican rum	1 part Benedictine
1 part cherry brandy	Club soda

Pour rum, cherry brandy, and Benedictine over 1 large ice cube in a sling glass or 12-ounce tumbler. Stir. Fill glass with chilled soda. Decorate with a spiral-cut peel of lime.

Trader Vic Rum Fizz

1½ ounces light Puerto Rican rum	2 teaspoons bar sugar
1 ounce lemon juice	1 egg
	½ ounce cream soda

Shake in a commercial electric drink mixer (or in a shaker can with mixing glass) with ice cubes. Strain into fizz glass. Sprinkle with grated orange peel.

·HOT·RUM·DRINKS·
FROM THE COLD COUNTRIES

American Grog

1 ounce dark Jamaica rum	Juice of ½ lemon
2 lumps sugar	1 lemon slice
2 whole cloves	Boiling water
1 cinnamon stick	

Mix all ingredients except water in a heated mug. Fill with boiling water and stir well.

Auld Man's Milk

2 ounces light Puerto Rican rum	1 teaspoon bar sugar
2 ounces brandy	1 glassful of milk, heated to
1 whole egg	boiling

Shake in a preheated shaker. Pour into a hot glass and dust with grated nutmeg.

Black Stripe

This is an old one, one of the first rum drinks I ever made. It's good for a cold, good for everything.

2 maraschino cherries	2 whole cloves
1 teaspoon honey	1 stick cinnamon
Boiling water	¼ ounce 151-proof rum
1 ounce dark Jamaica rum	

Crush cherries in bottom of a heatproof mug or glass. Add honey and boiling water to fill; stir. Add Jamaica rum, cloves, and cinnamon. Float 151-proof rum. Flame.

Bumpo

Juice of 1 lime or of ½ lemon	Bar sugar to taste
3 ounces Barbados or Trinidad	Boiling water
rum	

Put lime or lemon juice, rum, and sugar in a heavy pewter or earthenware mug. Fill with boiling water. Stir. Dust with grated nutmeg.

Café au Rhum

Add ¾ ounce light Puerto Rican rum to 1 cup hot coffee.

Café Brûlot Antoine

6 cocktail sugar cubes
Spiral-cut peel of 1 lemon
2 sticks cinnamon
4 whole cloves

4 ounces light Puerto Rican rum
Strong hot coffee to fill 4
   demitasse cups

Put sugar, lemon peel, cinnamon, cloves, and rum into a chafing dish set over a low flame. When warm, ignite. Ladle the flaming brew for 1 minute, then gradually extinguish by pouring in coffee. Ladle into demitasse cups. Makes 4 servings.

Café Prado

1 tablespoon granulated sugar
8 ounces black coffee
¼ cup semisweet chocolate bits
⅛ teaspoon ground cinnamon

2 cups hot (not boiled) milk
1½ to 2 ounces light rum
½ cup sweetened whipped cream

Stir sugar into coffee and heat. Add chocolate and cinnamon and stir over low heat until chocolate melts. Add milk. Whip until frothy. Pour into preheated cups. Add about 2 teaspoons rum to each cup. Top with whipped cream. Makes 4 to 6 servings.

Café Royale

1 demitasse cup of strong hot
   coffee

1 cocktail sugar cube
Demerara rum

Place a teaspoon over a demitasse cup of coffee. Put sugar in teaspoon. Fill teaspoon with rum. Light rum. When flame dies, pour contents of spoon into coffee and stir. VARIATION: Omit sugar; simply flame a spoonful of rum.

Café San Juan (hot)

1 quart very strong hot coffee
1 teaspoon whole cloves
1 stick cinnamon
12 cocktail sugar cubes
Grated peel of 1 orange

¾ cup Trader Vic Rum and
  Brandy mix (or use half light
  Puerto Rican rum and half
  brandy)

Put coffee, cloves, cinnamon, sugar, and orange peel into chafing dish. Heat thoroughly. Pour a little of the rum and brandy into a ladle and ignite it over the chafing dish; pour into coffee and spoon the coffee over and over. Continue adding the rest of the rum and brandy in the same way—burning it for a moment before dipping into the chafing dish. Dip and ladle until flame dies. Ladle into demitasse cups. Makes 1 quart.

Chocolate Coffee

2 ounces unsweetened chocolate
1 cup strong hot coffee
2 tablespoons bar sugar
Pinch of salt

3 cups scalded hot milk
4 ounces light Puerto Rican rum
Whipped cream

In a saucepan, stir chocolate with coffee until melted. Add sugar, salt, and hot milk. Beat until frothy. Stir in rum. Pour into 4 mugs. Top each with whipped cream.

Coffee Grog—1

1 teaspoon Hot Buttered Rum
  Batter (see Index)
1 strip lemon peel
1 strip orange peel

1½ ounces light Puerto Rican
  rum
1 ounce fresh cream
Hot black coffee

Put batter, lemon peel, orange peel, and rum into a preheated mug. Stir. Add cream. Fill mug with coffee.

Coffee Grog—2

2 whole cloves	¾ ounce 151-proof Demerara
1 orange twist	rum
1 lemon twist	Hot black coffee
¼ ounce Grand Marnier	3 teaspoons Lopez coconut cream

Heat and flame cloves, orange twist, lemon twist, Grand Marnier, and rum in a Pyrex saucepan or in the blazer pan of a chafing dish. Fill headhunter mug ¾ full of hot coffee; stir in coconut cream. Spoon flaming mixture on top of coffee. Decorate with an 8-inch cinnamon stick.

Hot Brown Cow

3 ounces hot milk	2 ounces dark Jamaica rum
3 ounces strong hot coffee	

Pour milk and coffee into an 8-ounce highball glass or mug. Add rum and stir. Dust with grated nutmeg if you wish.

Hot Buttered Rum

3 or 4 whole cloves	1½ ounces light Puerto Rican
1 heaping teaspoon Hot Buttered	rum
Rum Batter (recipe below)	Boiling water

Preheat a skull mug or other 6-ounce heatproof mug with boiling water. Put cloves and batter into mug. Add rum. Fill mug with hot water. Stir well. Hit with a hot poker. Decorate with an 8-inch cinnamon stick.

Hot Buttered Rum Batter

1 pound brown sugar	¼ to ½ teaspoon ground cloves
¼ pound soft butter	Pinch of salt
¼ to ½ teaspoon ground nutmeg	
¼ to ½ teaspoon ground cinnamon	

Beat sugar and butter together until thoroughly creamed and fluffy. Beat in nutmeg, cinnamon, cloves, and salt. Makes about 2½ cups.

Hot Buttered Rum Cow

1 teaspoon Hot Buttered Rum Batter (see Index)	**½ ounce Jamaica rum**
1½ ounces light Puerto Rican rum	**Hot milk**

Put batter and rums into a preheated mug. Stir well. Fill mug with hot milk. Stir. Dust with grated nutmeg.

Hot Rum Cow

1 to 1½ ounces light Puerto Rican rum	**1 dash Angostura bitters**
1 teaspoon bar sugar	**1 dash vanilla**
	8 ounces very hot milk

Blend thoroughly in an electric drink mixer. Pour into a large heated mug or a planter's punch glass or tall tumbler. Dust with grated nutmeg.

Hot Rum Punch

2 cocktail sugar cubes	**4 ounces light Puerto Rican rum**
Boiling water	**4 dashes Angostura bitters**

Dissolve sugar in a little hot water in a preheated punch glass. Add rum, bitters, and a slice of lemon or lime. Fill glass with hot water. Dust with grated nutmeg.

Hot Rum Sling

2 cocktail sugar cubes	**Juice of ½ lemon**
Boiling water	**2 ounces Jamaica rum**
1 dash Angostura bitters	

Dissolve sugar in a little boiling water in a mug. Add bitters, lemon juice, rum, and boiling water to fill mug. Stir.

Icebreaker

1 teaspoon sugar
1 cup very hot tea
1 cinnamon stick or ¼ teaspoon
  ground cinnamon

1½ ounces Barbados rum

Stir together in a mug.

Jamaica Dickens

½ ounce lemon or lime juice
½ ounce Simple Syrup (see
  Index)

1½ ounces dark Jamaica rum
2 ounces boiling water
5 whole cloves

Stir together in a preheated mug the lemon or lime juice, syrup, and rum. Add water and cloves. Stir.

Mulled Cider

If you like a sweeter drink, add sugar to cider during heating.

1 quart hard cider
6 whole cloves

Grated nutmeg
Cognac or rum

Heat cider with cloves and a little nutmeg; do not allow to boil. Ladle into mugs. Add to each mug a splash of cognac or rum and a cinnamon stick. Makes about 6 servings.

Northwest Passage

3 or 4 whole cloves
1 barspoon Hot Buttered Rum
  Batter (see Index)

1 ounce 151-proof Demerara
  rum
Boiling water

Put cloves, batter, and rum into a skull mug. Fill with boiling water. Stir well. Hit with a hot poker. Add an 8-inch cinnamon stick.

Rum and Coffee

Add 1 ounce Barbancourt 5-star rum to a demitasse cup of hot coffee. Or add 1½ ounces Barbancourt 3-star rum to a large cup of American-style coffee. Add sugar to taste.

Rum Toddy (hot)—1

1 teaspoon bar sugar
5 ounces boiling water
1½ ounces light Puerto Rican
   rum

1 lemon slice studded with cloves

Dissolve sugar in 1 ounce of the boiling water in a preheated mug. Add rum, lemon slice, 4 ounces boiling water, and a cinnamon stick.

Rum Toddy (hot)—2

1 cocktail sugar cube
Boiling water

2 ounces light Puerto Rican rum

Put sugar into a whiskey glass or mug. Fill ⅔ full with boiling water. Add rum. Stir. Decorate with a lemon slice. Dust with grated nutmeg.

Skull and Bones

2 whole cloves
1 barspoon Hot Buttered Rum
   Batter (see Index)

1 ounce dark Jamaica rum
Hot water

Put cloves, batter, and rum in a skull mug. Fill mug with hot water. Stir. Decorate with an 8-inch cinnamon stick. Hit with a hot poker.

Tahitian Coffee

This is my own adaptation of Irish coffee.

1 jar (1 pound) Mandalay coconut
   syrup
1 tablespoon instant coffee
   powder

1 pint heavy (whipping) cream
1 teaspoon instant coffee powder
Hot black coffee
Golden rum

Stir together coconut syrup and the 1 tablespoon instant coffee to make base mix. Beat together cream and the 1 teaspoon instant coffee until softly whipped to make cream topping. To prepare each drink: Preheat a fizz glass with hot water; empty. Put 1 level teaspoon of the base mix into the glass. Add coffee to fill glass to within ½ inch of top. Stir. Add 1 ounce golden rum. Float cream topping on top of drink.

Tom and Jerry (using prepared batter)

1 heaping dessert spoon Tom and
  Jerry Quantity Batter (recipe
  below)
½ ounce dark Jamaica rum

½ ounce brandy
Boiling water, hot coffee, or hot
  milk

Preheat a 6-ounce Tom and Jerry mug with hot water. Add batter, rum, and brandy and stir. Fill mug with boiling water, hot coffee, or hot milk. Stir.

Tom and Jerry Quantity Batter

12 eggs, separated
3½ pounds bar sugar
½ teaspoon ground nutmeg

½ teaspoon ground cinnamon
¼ teaspoon ground cloves
¼ teaspoon cream of tartar

Beat egg yolks with 3 pounds of the sugar and the nutmeg, cinnamon, and cloves until thick and light. Separately, beat egg whites with cream of tartar until soft peaks form; gradually beat in remaining sugar; beat until stiff. Gently fold whites into yolks.

Tom and Jerry (single drink)

1 egg, separated
1 teaspoon bar sugar
1 ounce dark Jamaica rum

¼ teaspoon ground allspice
Hot water
¼ ounce brandy

Beat egg yolk with sugar, rum, and allspice until smooth and thick. Separately, beat egg white until stiff. Fold white into yolk mixture. Put mixture into a preheated mug. Add hot water to fill mug ¾ full. Stir gently. Add brandy. Dust with grated nutmeg.

Whaler's Toddy (hot)

1 teaspoon bar sugar   2 whole cloves
4 ounces boiling water   2 ounces dark Jamaica rum
½ lemon slice

Dissolve sugar in water in an 8-ounce mug. Add lemon, cloves, and rum. Stir. Sprinkle with grated fresh nutmeg.

JASPER'S JAMAICAN DRINKS

Montego Bay, Jamaica, is renowned resort territory. So almost everybody who makes drinks there makes drinks like nothing else in this stinkin' world. But as in every place, there is always one guy who does it better than anyone else. And when Shirley Sarvis went out researching rum drinks for me, she found out that in Montego Bay—in fact, in all of Jamaica—that guy is Jasper LeFranc. Everyone told Sarvis to go see Jasper at the Bay Roc Hotel. If she asked the mayor or the postman or the city jailer or even the rum executives in Kingston city, they all said to go see Jasper LeFranc. So she went to see Jasper LeFranc.

He turned out to be a tall fellow. And Sarvis said that he looked a little like an American Indian. He was just one peaches 'n' cream guy—soft-spoken and wonderful—and he gave us a lot of his very own original recipes. Here they are.

Jasper's jigger is 1¼ ounces. His light-colored Jamaica rum is one such as Appleton Special.

Basic Stock Mix

1 bottle (fifth) sweetened lime juice (squeeze fresh lime juice and add bar sugar to taste)

1¼ ounces Angostura bitters
½ teaspoon grated fresh nutmeg

Shake together very well and chill. Shake before using each time.

Bay Roc Special

1 jigger light Jamaica rum
⅓ jigger Drambuie

⅔ jigger Basic Stock Mix (recipe above)

Shake in an electric drink mixer with ice cubes. Strain into a chilled cocktail glass. Decorate with a maraschino cherry.

Frozen Eskimo

1 jigger 151-proof white rum
½ ounce Triple Sec

½ jigger sweetened fresh lime juice (sweeten juice to taste with bar sugar)

Blend with 2 cups shaved ice in an electric drink mixer to a frappé. Pile high in a 13-ounce balloon goblet. Decorate with a strawberry.

Jasper's Arawak Cocktail

1 jigger Myers's dark Jamaica rum
½ ounce Basic Stock Mix (see Index)

½ ounce honey

Shake in an electric drink mixer with ice cubes. Strain into a chilled cocktail glass.

Jasper's Jamaican

1 jigger light Jamaica rum
½ ounce sweetened fresh lime juice (sweeten juice to taste with bar sugar)

½ ounce pimiento liqueur

Shake in an electric drink mixer with ice cubes. Strain into a chilled cocktail glass.

Jasper's Rum Cocktail

1 jigger light Jamaica rum
⅓ jigger Cherry Herring

⅔ jigger Basic Stock Mix (see Index)

Shake in an electric drink mixer with ice cubes. Strain into a chilled cocktail glass. Decorate with a maraschino cherry.

Mona Cane

1 ounce Appleton Special rum
½ ounce Rumona liqueur

½ ounce Basic Stock Mix (see Index)

Shake in an electric drink mixer with ice cubes. Strain into a chilled cocktail glass. Decorate with a maraschino cherry.

Mule Shoe

1 jigger 151-proof white rum
½ ounce Triple Sec
½ ounce cherry brandy

⅔ jigger Basic Stock Mix (see Index)

Shake in an electric drink mixer with ice cubes. Strain into a chilled cocktail glass.

White Lightning

1 jigger 151-proof white rum
1 ounce Triple Sec

⅔ jigger sweetened fresh lime juice (sweeten juice to taste with bar sugar)

Shake in an electric drink mixer with ice cubes. Strain into a chilled cocktail glass. Decorate with a maraschino cherry.

Witch Doctor

1 jigger light Jamaica rum
⅓ jigger Cointreau
⅓ jigger cherry brandy

⅔ jigger Basic Stock Mix (see Index)

Shake in an electric drink mixer with ice cubes. Strain into a chilled cocktail glass. Decorate with a maraschino cherry.

JULEPS AND MOJITOS

Jamestown Julep

Mint sprigs
1 teaspoon bar sugar

Light Puerto Rican rum

In a tall highball glass, bruise 12 young mint sprigs with sugar. Add enough water to dissolve sugar and muddle lightly. Pack glass full with shaved ice. Fill glass with rum. Stir until glass is frosted. Store in refrigerator or bury is shaved ice for 1 hour. Decorate with additional mint sprigs. Serve with straws.

Manila Hotel Julep

½ tablespoon bar sugar
2 tablespoons water
Mint sprigs

4 ounces Bourbon or rye
2 teaspoons Barbados rum

In a tall chilled highball glass, dissolve sugar in water. Add 2 mint sprigs and muddle. Pack ⅓ of the glass with shaved ice, add 2 more mint sprigs, and muddle. Add shaved ice to fill glass ⅔ full, add 2 more mint sprigs, and muddle. Add shaved ice to fill glass. Add

Bourbon, then rum. Garnish with more mint. Spike with 2 spears of fresh ripe pineapple. Chill until frosted. Serve with straws.

Mojito—1

½ lime	2 ounces light Puerto Rican rum
1 teaspoon bar sugar	1 dash club soda
Mint sprigs	

Squeeze lime juice into a 10-ounce glass; save spent shell. Add sugar and 3 mint sprigs and muddle. Fill glass with shaved ice. Add rum. Stir or swizzle until glass frosts. Add soda. Garnish with the spent lime shell and additional mint. Serve with straws.

Mojito—2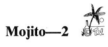

½ teaspoon bar sugar	2 ounces light Puerto Rican rum
6 or 7 mint sprigs	1 dash dark Jamaica rum

Fill planter's punch glass half full of shaved ice. Add sugar and mint sprigs. Bruise mint on ice with a stirrer or muddler. Fill glass with shaved ice. Add light rum. Stir thoroughly. Float Jamaica rum. Decorate with a fresh mint sprig dusted with bar sugar.

Mojito Criollo

1 lemon	2 ounces light Puerto Rican rum
1 teaspoon bar sugar	Club soda
6 mint sprigs	

Cut lemon in half; squeeze juice into an 8-ounce glass; add spent shells. Add sugar and mint. Muddle. Fill glass with shaved ice. Add rum. Stir well. Fill glass with soda. Garnish with mint. Serve with straws.

Rum Julep—1

1 ounce bar sugar	3 ounces light Puerto Rican rum
Mint sprigs	

Half fill a 12-ounce glass with shaved ice. Add sugar, 5 mint sprigs, and rum; muddle thoroughly. Fill glass with shaved ice. Stir with up-and-down motion until glass is frosted. Decorate with more mint and a lemon slice. Serve with straws.

Rum Julep—2

8 mint sprigs	Juice of ½ lime
1 ripe freestone peach, peeled, halved, and pitted	1 teaspoon bar sugar
	5 ounces light Puerto Rican rum

Half fill a large goblet with shaved ice. Add 4 mint sprigs and muddle. Stand peach halves upright in center of glass; pack in place with shaved ice. Stir together lime juice, sugar, and rum; pour over ice. Chill until frosted. Garnish with 4 more mint sprigs. Serve with short straws.

Rum Julep—3

2 teaspoons Simple Syrup (see Index)	2 or 3 ounces light Puerto Rican rum
10 to 12 tender mint sprigs	1 teaspoon dark Jamaica rum
2 dashes Angostura bitters	

Put syrup, mint, and bitters in a mixing glass; bruise mint lightly with a muddler; then gently stir the 3 ingredients together for several minutes. Add 2 ounces of the light rum and stir thoroughly. Strain mint mixture into a chimney glass packed with shaved ice. Stir with an up-and-down motion for a few minutes. Add more shaved ice. Fill glass to within ¼ inch of top with more light rum. Repeat up-and-down stirring until glass is well frosted. Float Jamaica rum on top. Serve with straws.

Santiago Julep

Mint sprigs	1 ounce pineapple juice
¼ ounce grenadine	4 ounces light Puerto Rican rum
Juice of 1 large lime	

Bruise 6 mint sprigs with a little shaved ice in a 12-ounce glass. Pack glass with shaved ice. Add remaining ingredients. Stir. Chill until glass frosts. Decorate with additional mint sprigs. Serve with straws.

LOUSY RUM DRINKS

When you write a drink book, you are expected to tell about nearly all the drinks that you've heard about. There are bound to be some lousy drinks among them. So here are some of those. They might be beautiful to somebody, but to me they are lousy.

Blue Dame

⅔ ounce Barbancourt 5-star
  rum
⅔ ounce blue curaçao

⅔ ounce lime juice
1 egg white

Shake well with shaved ice. Strain into a large chilled cocktail glass.

Bluebeard's Wench

Who the hell would have blue curaçao?

1½ ounces light Virgin Islands
  rum
½ ounce blue curaçao

½ ounce Cointreau
½ ounce lemon juice

Shake with ice cubes. Strain into a chilled cocktail glass. Decorate with a maraschino cherry.

Don't Stop the Carnival

½ ounce light Virgin Islands rum
½ ounce 151-proof Virgin
  Islands rum
½ ounce dark Virgin Islands rum
½ ounce Falernum

¼ ounce Cointreau
1 dash green crème de menthe
Juice of ½ lemon
½ peeled ripe banana

Blend with 1 scoop shaved ice until frozen. Pour into a chilled 10-ounce glass. Decorate with an orange slice and a maraschino cherry.

Golden Gate

Terrible drink. But you hear about it.

1 part dry sherry
5 parts light Puerto Rican rum

Stir very well with ice cubes. Strain into a chilled cocktail glass. Add a twist of lemon peel.

Punch à la Romaine

2 pounds bar sugar
Juice of 10 lemons
Juice of 2 oranges
Spiral-cut peel of 1 orange
10 egg whites

1 bottle (fifth) light Puerto Rican
rum
1 bottle (fifth) dry white table
wine

Dissolve sugar in lemon and orange juice. Add orange peel and muddle well. Strain into punch bowl. Embed bowl in ice cubes to chill thoroughly. Beat egg whites until soft peaks form and turn into punch bowl. Stir. Pour in chilled rum and chilled wine. Serve in punch cups or wine glasses. Makes 12 servings.

Raspberry Blush

1 ounce Barbancourt 5-star or
Barbados rum
½ ounce dry vermouth

Juice of 1 lime
Raspberry syrup

Shake rum, vermouth, lime juice, and 1 generous dash of raspberry syrup with ice cubes. Strain into a chilled cocktail glass. Add a float of raspberry syrup.

Rum Scaffa

1 ounce light Puerto Rican rum
1 ounce Benedictine

1 dash Angostura bitters

Shake with ice cubes. Strain into a large chilled cocktail glass.

Yard of Flannel

1 egg   **Grating of fresh nutmeg**
2 ounces dark Jamaica rum   **1 12-ounce bottle ale**
1 tablespoon bar sugar

Beat together well the egg, rum, sugar, and nutmeg. Heat ale just to boiling point, then pour slowly into egg mixture, beating constantly to prevent curdling. Pour mixture back and forth between 2 large mugs until well aerated and smooth.

PUNCHES, COOLERS, AND BUCKETS FULL OF RUM PUNCH

Amber Rum Punch

¾ cup bar sugar
6 ounces pineapple juice
Juice of 6 oranges
Juice of 6 lemons

1 bottle (fifth) light Puerto Rican rum
1 bottle (about 1 quart) ginger ale or club soda, chilled

In a large punch bowl, dissolve sugar in pineapple, orange, and lemon juice. Add rum. Add a large block of ice and let chill. At serving time, add ginger ale or soda and garnish with sliced pineapple, oranges, cherries, and/or other fruits in season. Makes about 18 servings.

Arrack Cooler

1½ ounces arrack
1 teaspoon Simple Syrup
½ ounce light Puerto Rican rum

1 teaspoon lemon juice
Club soda
1 dash champagne

Shake arrack, syrup, rum, and lemon juice with ice cubes. Strain into a goblet. Add a large ice cube. Fill with soda. Add champagne.

Bali Punch

1½ ounces light Puerto Rican rum
Juice of ½ lime

1 teaspoon bar sugar
½ ounce passion fruit juice

Shake with ice cubes. Strain into a 10-ounce glass. Fill glass with shaved ice. Decorate with fruit and a mint sprig. Serve with straws.

Bamboo Punch

1 ounce Trader Vic light Puerto Rican rum
1¼ ounces Trader Vic Mai Tai rum

Juice of 1 lime
2 dashes Peychaud bitters
½ ounce passion fruit nectar
1 dash rock candy syrup

Blend with ½ scoop shaved ice in an electric drink mixer. Serve in a bamboo cup with ice cubes to fill. Decorate with fresh mint and a fruit stick.

Barbados Punch

½ lime	1 dash rock candy syrup
½ ounce lemon juice	1½ ounces Barbados rum
1 dash grenadine	2 ounces club soda

Squeeze lime juice into a mixing glass; save shell. Add remaining ingredients, mix, and serve in a 10-ounce pilsner glass over ice cubes. Decorate with the spent lime shell, fresh mint, and a fruit stick.

Barbancourt Cassis Punch

⅔ cup crème de cassis	Club soda or champagne,
1 pint Barbancourt 5-star rum	chilled
1 cup dry vermouth	

Combine cassis, rum, and vermouth in a large pitcher and chill. Just before serving, pour over a block of ice in a punch bowl and add soda or champagne to taste. Makes about 12 servings.

Barbancourt Far North Punch

1 bottle (fifth) Barbancourt 5-star rum	1 cup maple syrup
	1 cup lime juice
2 ounces Cointreau	⅓ cup lemon juice

Mix all ingredients well. Chill for 2 to 4 hours. Pour over a large block of ice in a punch bowl. Garnish with lime slices. To serve, pour over shaved ice in old-fashioned glasses. Makes about 25 servings.

Barbancourt Fruit Punch

1 bottle (fifth) Barbancourt 5-star rum	1 pint orange juice
	1 cup pineapple juice
½ cup Grand Marnier	1 cup lemon juice

Stir all ingredients together and chill. Pour over a block of ice in a bowl. Garnish with orange slices. Makes about 10 servings.

Barbancourt Rum Cup

1 bottle (fifth) Barbancourt 5-star rum	⅔ cup lime juice
2 dashes Angostura bitters	⅔ cup orgeat syrup

Combine all ingredients in a pitcher and chill. At serving time, pour over a block of ice in a punch bowl. Makes about 10 servings. VARIATION: Add chilled club soda to taste.

Bengal Lancers' Punch

1 cup bar sugar	3 ounces curaçao
½ cup orange juice	1 bottle (fifth) claret
½ cup pineapple juice	1 pint club soda, chilled
½ cup lemon juice	1 bottle (fifth) champagne, chilled
3 ounces Barbados rum	

Combine sugar and fruit juices in a punch bowl and stir until sugar is dissolved. Stir in rum and curaçao. Add a large block of ice. Add chilled claret. Let stand until thoroughly chilled. At serving time, add soda and champagne. Garnish with fresh fruits in season and mint sprigs. Serve in punch cups or champagne glasses. Makes 10 servings.

Best Punch

1 ounce Jamaica rum	Juice of 2 lemons
1 ounce curaçao	1 tablespoon bar sugar
2 ounces brandy	1 bottle (fifth) champagne, chilled
1 cup strong tea	1 quart club soda, chilled

Mix all ingredients except champagne and soda in punch bowl. Add a large block of ice; chill thoroughly. At serving time, add champagne and soda. Makes 10 servings.

Bishop's Cooler

½ lemon	3 ounces burgundy
½ orange	½ ounce Jamaica rum
1 teaspoon bar sugar	

Squeeze lemon and orange over ice cubes in a 10-ounce glass; add sugar and stir. Add burgundy and stir. Float the rum.

Boston Cooler—1

Juice of ½ lemon
¼ teaspoon sugar

2 ounces dark New England or
    Jamaica rum
Club soda

Shake lemon juice, sugar, and rum with ice cubes. Strain into a highball glass. Fill with soda.

Boston Cooler—2

2 ounces cognac
½ teaspoon lemon juice
½ teaspoon sugar

Club soda
1 dash Jamaica rum

Shake cognac, lemon juice, and sugar with ice cubes. Strain into a goblet. Add ice cubes. Fill with soda. Add rum.

Brandy Punch

1 pound bar sugar
Juice of 20 lemons
1½ quarts brandy
6 ounces curaçao

4 ounces Jamaica rum
2 ounces maraschino liqueur
1 quart club soda, chilled

Dissolve sugar in lemon juice in a punch bowl. Add a large block of ice and brandy, curaçao, rum, and maraschino. Let chill. At serving time, add soda and sliced oranges and fruits in season. Serve in punch cups or wine glasses. Makes 15 servings.

Buddha Punch

1 bottle (fifth) dry white table
    wine
2 ounces orange juice
1 ounce curaçao

1 ounce light Puerto Rican rum
1 bottle (fifth) champagne, chilled
1 quart club soda, chilled

Mix wine, orange juice, curaçao, and rum in punch bowl. Add a large block of ice. Let chill. At serving time, add champagne and soda. Serve in champagne glasses. Makes 15 servings.

Cardinal Punch—1

1½ pounds bar sugar
2 quarts claret or other dry red
    table wine
1 pint brandy

1 pint Barbados rum
1½ ounces sweet vermouth
2 quarts club soda, chilled
1 split champagne, chilled

Dissolve sugar in a punch bowl with a little soda. Add chilled claret, brandy, rum, and vermouth. Add a large block of ice. Let chill. At serving time, add soda and champagne and sliced oranges and pineapple. Serve in wine glasses. Makes 20 servings.

Cardinal Punch—2

Juice of 12 lemons
Bar sugar
1 pint brandy
1 pint light Puerto Rican rum
½ pint sweet vermouth

2 quarts claret or other dry red
    table wine, chilled
1 quart carbonated water, chilled
1 bottle (tenth) champagne,
    chilled

In a punch bowl, stir lemon juice with enough sugar to sweeten until sugar is dissolved. Add brandy, rum, and vermouth. Add a large block of ice. Let chill. At serving time, add claret, carbonated water, and champagne. Serve in punch cups. Makes about 25 servings. VARIATION: Add 1 strained pot of tea.

Caribbean Punch

3 quarts light Puerto Rican rum
½ pint Jamaica rum
1 gallon water
1 pint lemon juice
4 ounces curaçao

3 oranges, sliced
1 large can sliced pineapple,
    drained
1 pint fresh raspberries
Falernum to taste

Mix all ingredients thoroughly and pour over a large block of ice in a punch bowl. Let chill until very cold before serving. Makes 25 servings.

Carolina Cup

1 quart medium rum such as   1 pint curaçao
  Siegert's Bouquet,   1 cup orange juice
  Barbancourt 5-star, or
  Barbados

Combine ingredients and pour over a large piece of ice in a punch
bowl. Let chill. Serve in chilled punch cups. Garnish each with a thin
orange slice. Makes about 15 servings.

Champagne Punch

½ pound bar sugar   8 ounces Haitian or light Puerto
1 quart strained green tea   Rican rum
1 small can (about 8 ounces)   1 pint brandy
  crushed pineapple   1 bottle (fifth) champagne, chilled

In a punch bowl, stir sugar in tea until dissolved. Add a large
block of ice, pineapple, rum, and brandy. Let chill. At serving time,
add champagne. Garnish with orange and lemon slices and mint
sprigs. Serve in champagne glasses. Makes 15 servings.

Cooper's Ranch Punch

2 ounces light Puerto Rican rum   ½ ounce pineapple juice
1 dash grenadine   Juice of ½ lime
2 ounces canned guava juice

Pour over ice cubes in a tall highball glass. Stir.

Cranberry House Cooler

1½ ounces Jamaica rum   Juice of 1 lime
3 dashes curaçao   1½ ounces pineapple juice
2 ounces cranberry juice   1½ ounces orange juice

Pour over ice cubes in a 12-ounce glass. Stir. Garnish with fresh
mint and an orange slice. Serve with straws.

Empire City Punch

4 lemons
2 oranges
½ pound cube sugar
2 bottles (1 quart each) club soda
2 ounces maraschino liqueur
2 ounces curaçao
2 ounces Benedictine
1 quart dark Jamaica rum,
  chilled
1 bottle cognac, chilled

4 bottles (fifths) tokay wine,
  chilled
4 fifths madeira wine, chilled
4 fifths claret or other dry red
  table wine, chilled
1 fresh ripe pineapple, peeled,
  cored, and diced
1 pint fresh strawberries, sliced
12 oranges, thinly sliced
6 fifths champagne, chilled

Rub the lemons and 2 oranges with cubes of sugar until all of the fruit color is absorbed by the sugar. In a large punch bowl, dissolve sugar in 1 bottle of soda. Add a large block of ice. Add maraschino, curaçao, Benedictine, rum, cognac, tokay, madeira, and claret. Add pineapple, strawberries, and sliced oranges. Let chill thoroughly. Just before serving, add remaining bottle of chilled soda and the champagne. Serve in punch glasses or champagne goblets. Makes 100 servings.

Fish House Punch, Barbancourt

3 bottles (fifths) Barbancourt
  3-star rum
½ pint Grand Marnier
1 pint lemon juice

1 cup lime juice
1 cup sugar
1 cup Falernum
1 quart strong tea

Combine all ingredients and chill for several hours. Pour over a large block of ice in a punch bowl. Makes about 24 servings.

Furnace Creek Cooler (Bakke Pushover)

1½ ounces light Puerto Rican
  rum
1½ ounces apple juice
1 dash lemon juice

1 dash lime juice
1 dash grenadine or maraschino
  liqueur
Club soda, chilled

Shake all ingredients except soda with ice cubes. Strain into a 12-

ounce glass. Add 1 ice cube. Fill with soda. Garnish with fruits in season.

Golden Rum Punch

1 fifth golden Puerto Rican rum, chilled
4 ounces apricot liqueur
1 pint unsweetened grapefruit juice

½ pint pineapple juice
Juice of 2 to 3 lemons
1 quart club soda, chilled

Pour rum, apricot liqueur, grapefruit juice, pineapple juice, and lemon juice over a large block of ice in a chilled punch bowl. Stir to mix. At serving time, add soda. Float thin orange slices or 2 cans drained, partly thawed frozen pineapple chunks. Makes 25 to 30 servings.

Gun Club Punch—1

1 ounce light Puerto Rican rum
1 ounce dark Jamaica rum
1 dash grenadine
1 dash curaçao

Juice of 1 lime
1½ ounces unsweetened pineapple juice

Blend with 1 scoop shaved ice in an electric drink mixer. Pour into a green big shot glass or large tumbler. Fill glass with ice cubes. Decorate with fresh mint and a fruit stick.

Gun Club Punch—2

1½ ounces light Puerto Rican rum
½ ounce 151-proof Demerara rum
1 dash curaçao

Juice of 1 lime
1½ ounces unsweetened grapefruit juice
1 dash rock candy syrup

Blend with 1 scoop shaved ice in an electric drink mixer. Pour into a red big shot glass or large tumbler. Fill glass with ice cubes. Decorate with fresh mint and a fruit stick.

Hana Punch

1½ ounces light Puerto Rican rum	½ ounce lemon juice
3 ounces pineapple juice	1 teaspoon bar sugar

Blend with 1 scoop shaved ice in an electric drink mixer. Serve in a tortuga or tall highball glass. Fill glass with ice cubes. Decorate with fresh mint.

Hawaiian Punch

2 ounces light Puerto Rican rum	Juice of ½ lemon
½ ounce curaçao	1 ounce orange juice
	1 teaspoon bar sugar

Shake with ice cubes. Pour into a 10-ounce glass. Garnish with fruit.

Ibo Lele Rhum Punch

A favorite drink with Louis A. Gardère of the Barbancourt rum family.

1½ ounces Barbancourt 5-star rum	Juice of 1 lime
½ ounce grenadine or Simple Syrup (see Index)	1 dash Angostura bitters

Stir with ice cubes in a tall glass. Decorate with a slice of pineapple, a slice of orange, and a maraschino cherry. Dust with grated nutmeg.

Jackstone Cooler

Spiral-cut lemon peel	Club soda
3 ounces Jamaica rum	

Drop lemon peel into a 12- to 14-ounce chimney glass with end hanging over edge of glass. Add 3 or 4 ice cubes and rum. Fill with soda. Stir.

John Merrill Punch

1¼ ounces dark Jamaica rum
2 ounces orange juice
½ ounce lemon juice

1 ounce frozen pineapple-
  grapefruit juice

Shake with ice cubes. Pour into a 10-ounce glass.

Kahala Cooler

½ lime
1 dash rock candy syrup
1 dash grenadine
¾ ounce Amer Picon

1 ounce pineapple juice
1 ounce brandy
1 ounce light Puerto Rican rum

Squeeze lime juice into mixing glass ¾ full of shaved ice; save lime shell. Add remaining ingredients. Shake. Pour into a 12-ounce glass. Add the spent lime shell.

Kava Bowl

1 ounce Siegert's Bouquet rum
6 ounces light Puerto Rican rum
1 ounce grenadine
2 ounces unsweetened pineapple
  juice

4 ounces lemon juice
1 ounce orgeat syrup

Blend with 3 scoops shaved ice in an electric drink mixer. Pour into a large scorpion bowl or wide-bowled goblet. Decorate with a gardenia. Serve with long straws.

Luau Punch

4 ounces golden Puerto Rican
  rum
1 can (1 pound, 4 ounces)
  pineapple chunks, drained
1 bottle (fifth) Bourbon

8 ounces pineapple juice
8 ounces grapefruit juice
4 ounces lemon juice
1 bottle (fifth) champagne

Pour rum over pineapple chunks and let stand, chilled, overnight. Next day, combine pineapple and rum with Bourbon, pineapple juice, grapefruit juice, and lemon juice in a large punch bowl. Chill in refrigerator for 1 hour. Just before serving, add a large block of ice. Add champagne and stir gently. Makes about 16 5-ounce servings.

Myrtle Bank Punch

1½ ounces 151-proof Demerara rum	6 dashes grenadine
Juice of ½ lime	1 teaspoon bar sugar
	Maraschino liqueur

Shake rum, lime juice, grenadine, and sugar with cracked ice. Strain over ice cubes in a 10-ounce glass. Add a float of maraschino. Serve with straws.

Navy Punch, Barbancourt

1 bottle (fifth) Barbancourt 5-star rum	½ cup lime juice
½ cup orange curaçao	½ cup sugar
1 pint lemon juice	Grated peel of 2 lemons
	Club soda

Stir all ingredients except soda together well. Pour over ice in a punch bowl. Add soda to taste (about 1 pint). Makes about 12 servings.

Nourmahal Punch

½ lime	2 dashes Angostura bitters
2 ounces light or dark Jamaica rum	Club soda

Squeeze lime over ice cubes in an old-fashioned glass; drop in the spent shell. Add rum and bitters. Stir. Fill glass with soda.

*

A lot of things can be simple and a lot of things can be complicated; but here is one that is simple.

After Sarvis was down in Trinidad, she came back with a wonderful story about a custom from the early colonial days of Trinidad which sounds like an oh-so-good-peachy thing to me. It was almost like a ritual.

On a Sunday morning about eleven o'clock, all the neighbors would congregate at the host plantation for tall Trinidad rum punches (see Ocean View Rum Punch, below) and oysters and asparagus roll-up sandwiches. The oysters were these little wood or tree oysters that grow in the mangrove thickets around the island and are simply terrific (at that time they weren't contaminated). They were served on the half shell with fresh limes on ice on giant silver platters. Each guest would eat a dozen or so. The sandwiches were the damnedest finger sandwiches you've ever eaten: each a cooked asparagus spear rolled up in paper-thin slices of light brown bread that had been spread with Angostura Bitters Butter Whip (recipe below). It all sounds simple and delicious.

Angostura Bitters Butter Whip

Beat ½ cup soft butter until creamy. Gradually beat in 1 tablespoon catsup, 1 teaspoon Angostura bitters, 1 teaspoon fresh lime juice, a pinch of salt, and a generous dash of Tabasco. Spread on paper-thin slices of light brown bread and roll around an asparagus spear. Makes ½ cup.

Ocean View Rum Punch

2 ounces Siegert's Bouquet or
    golden Barbados or Jamaica
    rum
½ ounce fresh lime juice
½ ounce Simple Syrup (see
    Index)
2 heavy dashes Angostura bitters

Pour into a 10-ounce old-fashioned glass filled with ice cubes. Stir well. Dust with freshly grated nutmeg. Decorate with a maraschino cherry and a mint sprig.

Old Navy Punch

1½ pounds bar sugar
12 ounces lemon juice
6 ounces orange juice
4 ounces peach brandy
1 bottle (fifth) 151-proof
    Demerara rum
1 pint brandy
3 bottles (tenths) champagne,
    chilled

Dissolve sugar in lemon and orange juice in a punch bowl. Add peach brandy, rum, and brandy. Add a large block of ice and let chill. At serving time, add champagne. Serve in champagne glasses. Makes 12 to 15 servings.

Old-fashioned Rum Punch

½ pint light Puerto Rican rum
½ pint peach brandy
½ pint lemon or lime juice

5 tablespoons Angostura bitters
3 quarts club soda

Stir together thoroughly in a punch bowl the rum, brandy, lemon or lime juice, and bitters. Add a large block of ice and let chill. At serving time, add soda. Makes 12 servings.

Orange Cup

16 ounces light Puerto Rican rum
1 bottle (fifth) dry white table
   wine

2 ounces Cointreau
Juice of 6 oranges, strained

Pour all ingredients over a large block of ice in a punch bowl. Stir well. Makes 12 servings.

Panorama Punch

¾ jigger light Puerto Rican rum
¾ jigger gin
½ jigger Cointreau

1 dash grenadine
Juice of ½ lime

Shake with ½ scoop ice cubes in a commercial electric drink mixer (or in a shaker can with mixing glass). Pour into a 10-ounce pilsner glass. Fill glass with ice cubes. Serve with a straw.

Pata Punch

1 ounce light Puerto Rican rum
1 ounce dark Jamaica rum
½ ounce curaçao
¼ ounce grenadine

1 ounce lemon juice
2 ounces orange juice
1 ounce pineapple juice

Pour over ice cubes in a double old-fashioned or a Mai Tai glass. Stir well.

Philadelphia Boating Punch

3 ounces golden Puerto Rican rum
1 ounce brandy

2 dashes lemon juice
2 dashes lime juice

Stir together in a tall glass. Fill glass with shaved ice. Decorate with fresh fruit. Serve with short straws.

Philippine Punch

1½ ounces light Puerto Rican rum
½ ounce Amer Picon
1 dash grenadine

2 ounces orange juice
1 ounce lemon juice
½ ounce passion fruit nectar

Blend in an electric drink mixer with 1 scoop shaved ice. Pour into a 12-ounce glass. Decorate with fresh mint or sliced fruit.

Pitcher Punch

1 part light Puerto Rican rum
1 part pineapple juice

1 part cranberry juice

Shake together. Pour over ice cubes. Decorate with sliced fresh fruit if you wish.

Plantation Punch

1½ ounces Southern Comfort
¾ ounce lemon juice
1 dash light Puerto Rican rum

1 teaspoon bar sugar
Club soda

Pour Southern Comfort, lemon juice, rum, and sugar over crushed ice in an old-fashioned glass. Stir well. Fill glass with soda. Add an orange slice and a maraschino cherry.

Planter's Punch, Trader Vic

In making a planter's punch, you've got to keep this in mind and thoroughly: Each different island has a rum of its own; and each island has a planter's punch of its own—built around its rum. There is no such thing as one proper planter's punch. There is one for Jamaica, one for Trinidad, one for Haiti, etc. (In the Caribbean a rum punch is usually considered the same thing as a planter's punch except that the rum punch does not have the club soda and the fresh fruit and mint decorations.)

But I will give you my formula. In it, you can substitute whatever rum you like best for the Jamaica. And you will have a fine drink. We must have sold at least a jillion of these.

½ lime
1 dash rock candy syrup
1 dash grenadine

1 ounce lemon juice
2 ounces dark Jamaica rum
2 ounces club soda

Squeeze lime juice over ice cubes in a planter's punch glass or 12½-ounce tumbler; save lime shell. Add remaining ingredients. Stir. Decorate with the spent lime shell, fresh mint, and a fruit stick.

Ponce Punch

½ bottle (fifth) light Puerto Rican rum
1 quart orange juice

1 pint pineapple juice
¾ ounce grenadine
Angostura bitters to taste

Stir vigorously with small ice cubes. Garnish with sliced fruit. Makes 10 servings.

Pondo Punch

3 ounces light Puerto Rican rum
½ ounce curaçao
¼ ounce grenadine

1 ounce orange juice
3 ounces club soda

Shake with ice cubes. Strain into a 14-ounce glass filled with shaved ice. Garnish with sliced fresh fruits.

Punch à la Marmora

1 pint orgeat syrup
3 ounces Simple Syrup (see Index)
4 ounces maraschino liqueur
4 ounces dark Jamaica rum
4 ounces cognac
2 lemons, sliced

2 oranges, sliced
1 small can (about 8 ounces)
  sliced pineapple
1 bottle (fifth) champagne, chilled
1 quart club soda, chilled

Mix orgeat, Simple Syrup, maraschino, rum, cognac, lemons, oranges, and pineapple in a punch bowl. Add a large block of ice. Let chill thoroughly. At serving time, pour in champagne and soda. Garnish with fresh fruits and berries in season. Serve in punch cups. Makes 15 servings.

Regent Punch—1

½ pound bar sugar
Juice of 5 lemons
2 ounces curaçao
2 ounces dark Jamaica rum
1 pint brandy

1 bottle (tenth) dry white table
  wine, chilled
1 pint club soda, chilled
1½ bottles (fifths) champagne,
  chilled

In a punch bowl, dissolve sugar in lemon juice. Stir in curaçao, rum, and brandy. Add a large block of ice. Let chill thoroughly. Add wine. At serving time, add soda and champagne. Decorate with fresh fruits and berries in season. Serve in punch cups. Makes 10 servings.

Regent Punch—2

18 cocktail sugar cubes
1 lemon, sliced
1 orange, sliced
1 small can (about 8 ounces)
  sliced pineapple with syrup

3 ounces dark Jamaica rum
6 ounces Bourbon
1 pint strong tea
1 bottle (fifth) champagne, chilled

In a punch bowl, dissolve sugar with lemons, oranges, and pineapple with syrup, muddling slightly. Add rum, Bourbon, and tea. Embed bowl in ice cubes to chill thoroughly. At serving time, add champagne. Serve in punch cups. Makes 8 to 10 servings.

Ruby Rum Punch

1 pint dark Jamaica rum	1 pint lemon juice
1 pint brandy	Bar sugar to taste
4 ounces curaçao	2 quarts sparkling red Concord
4 ounces yellow chartreuse	grape wine (Urbani or
4 ounces maraschino liqueur	Renault), well chilled
1 bottle (fifth) dry white table	1 quart club soda, well chilled
wine	

Thoroughly mix all ingredients except Concord grape wine and soda. Pour over a large block of ice in a punch bowl. Let chill. At serving time, add Concord grape wine and soda. Stir. Serve in punch cups or wine goblets. Makes 25 to 30 servings.

Rum and Tea Punch

1 quart boiling water	1½ pints light Puerto Rican rum
1 generous ounce tea leaves	¼ cup sweet sherry
1 pound bar sugar	1 cup lime juice

Pour water over tea and let steep for 10 minutes. Strain. Cool. Add sugar and stir until dissolved. Pour over a large block of ice in a punch bowl. Add rum, sherry, and lime juice. Stir well. Decorate with thin lime slices. Makes 12 servings.

Rum Cooler

2 ounces light Puerto Rican rum	1 dash Pernod or Herbsaint
1 ounce lime juice	Club soda, chilled
1 teaspoon grenadine	

Fill an 8-ounce highball glass halfway with shaved ice. Add rum, lime juice, grenadine, and Pernod or Herbsaint. Fill glass with soda. Stir well. Decorate with a fruit stick. Serve with straws.

Rum Fruit Punch

½ fresh pineapple, peeled, cored, and diced	1½ bottles (fifths) dark Jamaica rum
¾ cup Simple Syrup (see Index)	3 ounces peach brandy (optional)

1 cup lemon juice

1½ cups unsweetened pineapple
juice

2 quarts club soda, chilled

1 pint fresh strawberries, sliced

Place pineapple in a large pitcher. Stir in remaining ingredients except soda and strawberries. Chill thoroughly. At serving time, pour over a block of ice in a punch bowl. Add soda and strawberries. Makes 20 servings.

Rum Punch—1

1½ ounces light Puerto Rican
rum

1 teaspoon curaçao

½ teaspoon lemon juice

Club soda

Shake rum, curaçao, and lemon juice with ice cubes. Strain into a goblet. Add ice cubes. Fill glass with soda. Decorate with sliced fresh fruits. Serve with straws.

Rum Punch—2

12 lemons

2 cups bar sugar

1 quart strong hot tea

1 quart light, medium, or dark
Jamaica rum

Squeeze the juice from lemons; save rinds. Stir sugar with lemon juice to blend. Pour just-brewed tea, while very hot, over lemon rinds; let steep for 20 minutes; strain. Add strained tea to lemon juice; pour over a large block of ice in a punch bowl. Add rum. Serve in punch cups. Garnish each serving with a thin lemon slice. Makes 15 to 20 servings.

Rum Punch—3

1½ bottles (fifths) light Puerto
Rican rum

6 ounces pineapple juice

10 ounces orange juice

10 ounces lime juice

1½ quarts ginger ale or club soda

Combine rum and the pineapple, orange, and lime juice and allow to stand for 1 hour. Then pour over a block of ice in a large punch bowl. Let chill. At serving time, add chilled ginger ale or soda. Stir gently. Decorate with 1 pint sliced fresh strawberries and lemon and lime slices. Makes 12 servings.

St. Cecelia's Society Punch

1 fresh ripe pineapple, peeled, cored, and diced	1 quart brewed green tea
6 lemons, very thinly sliced	1 pint dark Jamaica rum
3 cups bar sugar	1 fifth peach brandy
1 bottle (fifth) brandy	4 fifths champagne, chilled
	4 quarts club soda, chilled

Combine pineapple, lemons, sugar, and brandy in a bowl; let stand overnight. Several hours before serving, add tea, rum, and peach brandy; pour over a large block of ice in a punch bowl. At serving time, add champagne and soda. Stir gently. Serve in champagne glasses or punch cups. Makes 50 servings.

Scorpion Punch

I was once invited to a cocktail party in Honolulu, and as I walked into the garden, somebody handed me a coconut filled with a Scorpion. The coconut was my only glass for the evening and the punch bowl was a barrel. Believe me, the thing was lively—try it at your next party.

1½ bottles (fifths) light Puerto Rican rum	½ pint orange juice
2 ounces gin	½ pint orgeat syrup
2 ounces brandy	1 bottle (tenth) dry white table wine
1 pint lemon juice	2 mint sprigs

Mix well all ingredients; pour over ice cubes in a punch bowl. Let stand for 2 hours. Add more ice. Garnish with gardenias. Serve in punch cups or coconut cups. Makes 12 servings.

Tahitian Rum Punch—1

½ lime	1 ounce Rhum St. James
1 dash rock candy syrup	

Squeeze lime juice over 1 large scoop shaved ice in mixing glass; save shell. Add syrup and rum. Shake. Pour into a parfait glass. Decorate with the spent lime shell and a maraschino cherry. Dust with grated nutmeg.

Tahitian Rum Punch—2

1½ ounces Rhum St. James	**½ lime**
1 teaspoon bar sugar	

Combine rum and sugar in mixing glass with a large ice cube; stir thoroughly. Squeeze lime juice over ice cubes in a 10-ounce glass; add the spent lime shell. Add mixed rum, sugar, and ice. Stir. Decorate with a banana, pineapple, or orange slice. Dust with grated nutmeg. Serve with straws.

Tahitian Rum Punch (quantity)

This is the original Tahitian Rum Punch recipe for large groups. It is a rigmarole but worth the trouble.

2 pounds brown sugar	**2 mint sprigs**
5 dozen oranges	**10 bottles (fifths) dry white table**
4 dozen lemons	**wine**
3 grapefruit	**6 fifths light Puerto Rican rum**
10 bananas	**1 fifth dark Jamaica rum**

Put sugar into a large crock. Squeeze juice from oranges, lemons, and grapefruit; add juices and all spent shells to crock. Slice in bananas. Add mint and wine. Let stand overnight. Next day, add the rums. Strain off and discard the fruit pulp and citrus shells. Stir punch well. Pour over a large block of ice in a punch bowl (or a barrel). Let mixture chill. Serve in punch cups or coconut cups. Makes about 100 servings.

Thanksgiving Punch

1 quart light Puerto Rican rum	**1 quart apple juice**
1 quart cranberry juice	**¼ cup lemon juice**

Pour over ice cubes in a large glass pitcher. Stir. Decorate with fruit slices if you wish. Makes 20 to 25 servings.

Tonga Punch

We used to sell this by the tons when we first started in business. It was one of the first drinks I originated. And it is still good.

2 ounces light Puerto Rican rum	**Juice of ½ lime**
1 dash grenadine	**1½ ounces orange juice**
½ ounce curaçao	**¾ ounce lemon juice**

Blend with ½ scoop shaved ice in an electric drink mixer. Pour into a 14-ounce optic chimney glass or other 14-ounce chimney glass. Decorate with fresh mint and a stirrer.

Tonga Punch (1 gallon)

32 ounces light Puerto Rican rum	**24 ounces orange juice**
8 ounces curaçao	**16 ounces lemon juice**
4 ounces grenadine	

Stir well with ice cubes. Pour over a large block of ice in a punch bowl. Serve in coconut cups or punch glasses. Makes 25 servings.

Tonga Punch (5 gallons)

5 quarts light Puerto Rican rum	**1 gallon orange juice**
20 ounces grenadine	**2½ quarts lemon juice**
1½ fifths curaçao	

Stir well with ice cubes. Pour over a large block of ice in a punch bowl. Serve in coconut cups or punch glasses. Makes 125 servings.

Trader Vic Punch

½ orange	**1 ounce dark Jamaica rum**
½ lemon	**1 dash orgeat syrup**
1 ounce light Puerto Rican rum	**1 dash rock candy syrup**

Squeeze orange juice over ½ scoop shaved ice in a double old-fashioned glass; drop shell in glass. Squeeze in lemon juice; drop in shell. Add remaining ingredients. Fill glass with shaved ice. Shake. Decorate with fresh mint and a fruit stick.

Trader Vic Rum Cup

1 orange	**2 ounces orange juice**
1 lemon	**1 ounce orgeat syrup**
1 lime	**1 ounce Siegert's Bouquet rum**
1 ounce lemon juice	**3 ounces light Puerto Rican rum**

Cut orange, lemon, and lime. Squeeze juice over 2 scoops shaved ice in container of an electric drink mixer; save shells. Add additional juice, orgeat, and rums. Blend. Pour into a large scorpion bowl or other large-bowled compote. Decorate with the spent orange, lemon, and lime shells. Serves 2.

Tutu Rum Punch

2 ounces dark Jamaica rum	**½ ounce Falernum**
¾ ounce frozen concentrated pineapple-grapefruit juice, undiluted	**½ ounce lemon juice**

Blend with ½ scoop shaved ice in an electric drink mixer. Pour into a Mai Tai (double old-fashioned) glass; add ice cubes. Decorate with a rock candy stick and fresh mint.

Water Isle Cooler

1½ ounces light Virgin Islands or Puerto Rican rum	**1 ounce orange juice**
1½ ounces coconut liqueur	**1 ounce pineapple juice**
½ ounce grenadine	**1 ounce grapefruit juice**

Shake with ice cubes. Pour into a 12-ounce glass. Decorate with an orange half slice and a maraschino cherry.

Yacht Club Punch

2 ounces light Puerto Rican rum
½ ounce grenadine
3 dashes Pernod or Herbsaint

1 teaspoon lemon juice
Club soda

Stir all ingredients except soda with ice cubes. Strain into a goblet. Add shaved ice and club soda to fill goblet. Garnish with sliced fruits in season. Serve with straws.

Zamboanga Punch

½ ounce light Puerto Rican rum
1½ ounces dark Jamaica rum
Juice of 1 lime

3 dashes Angostura bitters
1 dash grenadine
½ ounce passion fruit nectar

Blend with ½ scoop shaved ice in an electric drink mixer. Pour into a bamboo cup. Add ice cubes. Decorate with fresh mint and a fruit stick.

Zombies

2 bottles (fifths) dark Jamaica rum
4 bottles (fifths) light Puerto Rican rum
1 bottle (fifth) 151-proof Demerara rum

2 bottles curaçao
3 quarts lemon juice
3 quarts orange juice
1 quart grenadine
2 ounces Pernod or Herbsaint

Mix all ingredients thoroughly. Pour over a large block of ice in a punch bowl. Let chill thoroughly before serving, about 1 to 2 hours. Makes about 60 servings.

Barbados Red Rum Swizzle

½ lime
1 dash Angostura bitters

1 dash rock candy syrup
2 ounces Barbados rum

Squeeze lime juice into a Trader Vic sling glass or 12-ounce tumbler partly filled with shaved ice; save lime shell. Add bitters, syrup, and rum. Swizzle until drink is uniform. Decorate with the spent shell, fresh mint, and a fruit stick.

Bermuda Swizzle

2 ounces Trader Vic light Puerto
  Rican rum
2½ ounces Trader Vic Navy
  Grog mix

½ ounce apricot brandy

Pour into a planter's punch glass or 12½-ounce tumbler partly filled with shaved ice. Swizzle well. Decorate with a lime shell, a fresh mint sprig, and a fruit stick.

Caribbean Hot Swizzle

½ lime
¼ ounce rock candy syrup

1½ ounces dark Jamaica rum
Hot water

Squeeze lime juice into a 12-ounce glass; drop in spent lime shell. Add syrup and rum. Fill glass with hot water. Stir.

Kingston Swizzle

½ lime
1 teaspoon bar sugar

2 ounces dark Jamaica rum
Hot water

Squeeze lime juice into a 12-ounce glass; add spent shell. Add sugar and stir well. Add rum and enough hot water to nearly fill glass. Serve with swizzle stick.

Kona Swizzle

½ lime
½ ounce orgeat syrup

½ ounce Barbados rum
1 ounce Siegert's Bouquet rum

Squeeze lime juice into a 12-ounce sling or punch glass filled with shaved ice; save lime shell. Add orgeat and rums. Swizzle until drink is uniform. Decorate with the spent lime shell, fresh mint, and a fruit stick.

Martinique Swizzle

If you want a really good drink from the Caribbean that's *really* a drink from the Caribbean, you have it here.

½ lime
2 ounces Rhum St. James
1 dash Angostura bitters

1 dash rock candy syrup
1 dash Herbsaint

Squeeze lime juice into a 14-ounce chimney or highball glass filled with shaved ice; save shell. Add remaining ingredients. Swizzle until drink is uniform. Decorate with the spent lime shell, fresh mint, and a long stirrer.

Pineapple Rum Swizzle

2 ounces Barbancourt 5-star rum
3 ounces pineapple juice

¼ ounce grenadine or Simple Syrup (see Index)

Pour over shaved ice in a 10-ounce glass. Swizzle until thoroughly mixed.

Queen's Park Swizzle

This is from the Queen's Park Hotel in Trinidad.

½ lime	1 ounce 151-proof Demerara rum
1 ounce light Puerto Rican rum	1 dash Angostura bitters
1 ounce dark Jamaica rum	1 dash rock candy syrup

Squeeze lime juice into a 14-ounce chimney glass filled with shaved ice; save shell. Add remaining ingredients. Swizzle until uniform. Add the spent lime shell, fresh mint, and a swizzle stick or stirrer.

Rum Swizzle

2 ounces light Puerto Rican rum	1 teaspoon sugar
Juice of ½ lime	2 dashes bitters

Pour over 2 scoops shaved ice in a glass pitcher. Churn vigorously with a swizzle stick until the drink foams and pitcher frosts. Pour into a chilled highball glass. Decorate with a mint sprig.

Rum Swizzle (Bluebeard's Castle)

1½ ounces 151-proof Virgin Islands rum	½ ounce lemon juice
½ ounce Italian sweet vermouth	2 dashes Angostura bitters

Shake with ice cubes. Strain into a chilled old-fashioned glass. Sprinkle with grated nutmeg.

Trinidad Swizzle (Trinidad Hilton)

2 ounces Trinidad golden rum	1½ ounces mango juice
1 ounce vodka	½ ounce lime juice
2 dashes grenadine	¼ ounce Grand Marnier

Pour all ingredients except Grand Marnier over shaved ice in a tall serving glass. Stir. Add a swizzle stick. Float Grand Marnier on top. Decorate with a cherry, an orange slice, and a mint sprig. Drinker swizzles the drink.

AFTER DINNER DRINKS

Alexander Baby

1 ounce Barbados rum
1 ounce crème de cacao

1 ounce fresh cream

Shake with ice cubes. Strain into a chilled cocktail glass.

Gallant Knight

2 ounces Barbancourt 5-star rum
¼ ounce Grand Marnier

¼ ounce chartreuse
½ ounce lemon juice

Fill an old-fashioned glass with shaved ice. Pour ingredients into glass in order listed. Do not stir.

Gay Galliano

The Sandy Lane Hotel in Barbados sounds like a funny little place (I have a lot of sandy lane memories). But they tell me that it is the most elegant and delightful place on Barbados; I damn near fell out of my seat hearing that. Well, there is the nicest head bartender there by the name of Kermitt Beckles. He makes this drink. The name makes me laugh.

1½ ounces Mount Gay Barbados   **¾ ounce Galliano liqueur**
  rum   **½ ounce lime juice**

Blend with 1 small scoop shaved ice in an electric drink mixer until thick (semifrozen). Pour into a saucer champagne glass. Add a twist of lime peel.

Jamaica Snifter

1 ounce Jamaica rum   **1 ounce Trader Vic Navy Grog**
¼ ounce dark crème de cacao   **mix**
½ ounce passion fruit nectar

Pour into a mixing glass. Add 1 scoop of ice cubes. Hand-shake. Pour into an 11-ounce brandy snifter. Add ice if necessary. Garnish with a sprig of mint.

Rum Alexander

1½ ounces Barbancourt 5-star or   **1 ounce crème de cacao**
  Barbados rum   **1 ounce fresh cream**

Shake with ice cubes. Strain into a large chilled cocktail glass.

Rum Frappé

½ cup orange or lemon sherbet
1½ ounces dark Jamaica or Barbancourt 5-star rum

Put sherbet in a large saucer champagne glass. Gradually add rum, stirring slowly until smooth.

Rum Mocha

2 scoops vanilla ice cream   **Hot black coffee**
2 ounces light Puerto Rican rum

Half fill a 14-ounce glass with shaved ice. Add ice cream and rum. Fill glass with hot coffee. Stir.

Rum Sidecar

¾ ounce light Puerto Rican rum   **½ ounce lemon or lime juice**
¾ ounce Cointreau

Shake with ice cubes. Strain into a chilled cocktail glass which has been rimmed with sugar. VARIATION: Use equal parts of the 3 ingredients.

Trader Vic's After Dinner

½ ounce light Puerto Rican rum   **½ ounce evaporated milk**
1 ounce Grand Marnier

Shake with ice cubes. Strain into a chilled lady cocktail or other cocktail glass.

INDEX

400